It Happened In Maryland

It Happened In Maryland

Remarkable Events That Shaped History

Judy Colbert

gpp

Guilford, Connecticut

To buy books in quantity for corporate use
or incentives, call **(800) 962-0973**
or e-mail **premiums@GlobePequot.com.**

Map: Melissa Baker © Morris Book Publishing, LLC
Layout artist: Mary Ballachino
Project editor: Heather Santiago

Library of Congress Cataloging-in-Publication Data is available on file.
ISBN 978-0-7627-6970-4

Printed in the United States of America
10 9 8 7 6 5 4 3 2 1

CONTENTS

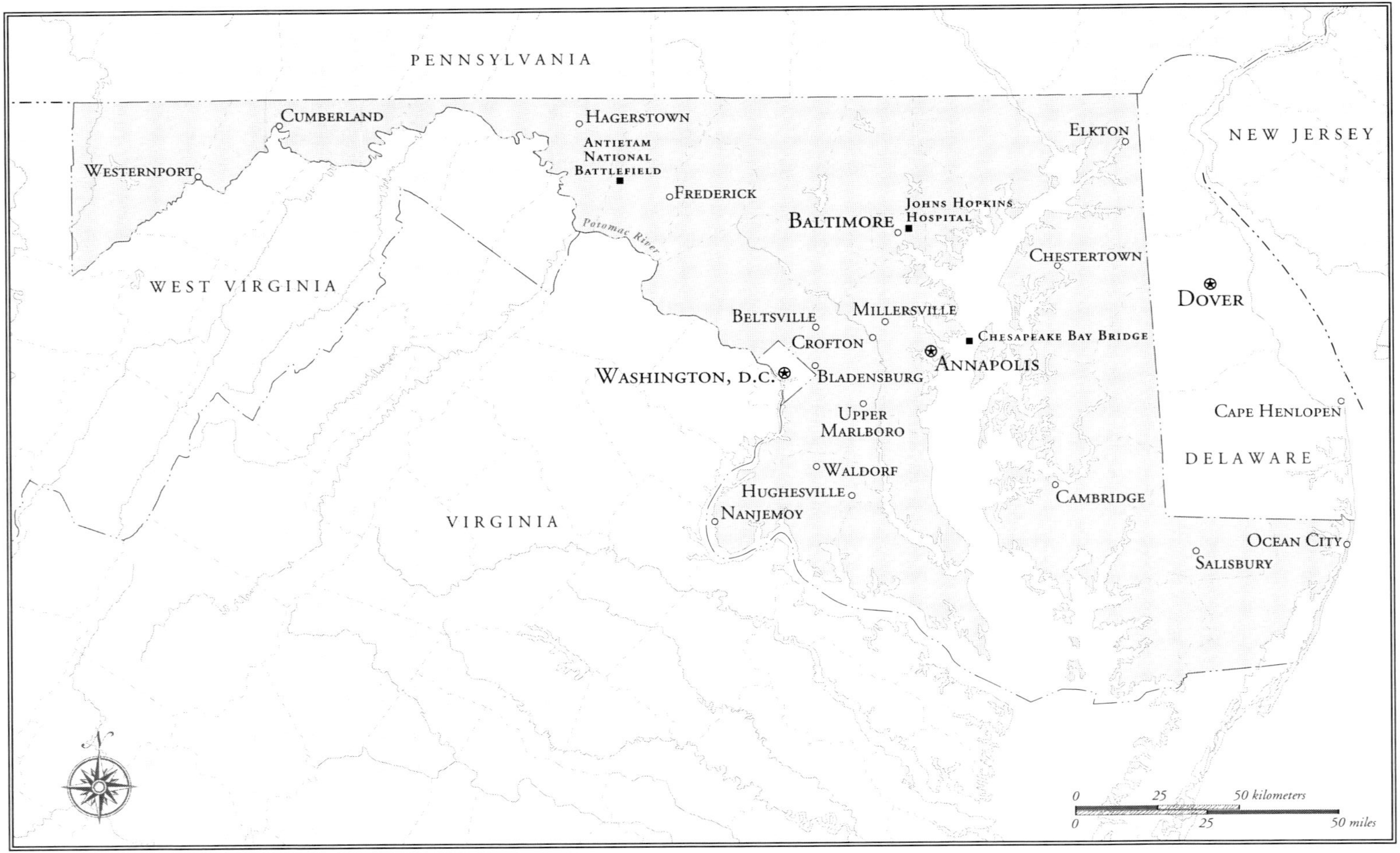

PENNSYLVANIA

NEW JERSEY

CUMBERLAND

WESTERNPORT

WEST VIRGINIA

VIRGINIA

HAGERSTOWN

ANTIETAM
NATIONAL
BATTLEFIELD

FREDERICK

Potomac River

ELKTON

CHESTERTOWN

JOHNS HOPKINS
HOSPITAL

BALTIMORE

MILLERSVILLE

BELTSVILLE

CROFTON

WASHINGTON, D.C.

BLADENSBURG

UPPER
MARLBORO

WALDORF

HUGHESVILLE

NANJEMOY

CHESAPEAKE BAY BRIDGE

ANNAPOLIS

DOVER

CAPE HENLOPEN

DELAWARE

OCEAN CITY

SALISBURY

CAMBRIDGE

0   25   50 miles

0   25   50 kilometers

MARYLAND

ACKNOWLEDGMENTS

This type of book cannot even begin to happen without help, guidance, support, and love from a lot of people. I'm sure I have forgotten a few people and I apologize. In the meantime, to the people I do remember, thank you: Joyce Stinnett Baki, Christine Bergmark, Troy Corley, Kathleen Crostic, Bob Cullen, James Dawson, Robert Devaney, Mike Dixon, Jill Feinberg, Francis B. Francois, Gerry Gaumer, Dr. Adam Goodheart, Liz Griffin, Dr. Jeannine Harter-Dennis, Gene Humphrey, Val Hymes, Warren Kahle, Jacques Kelly, Barry Kessler, Carolyn Laray, Kay MacIntosh, Kathy Mackel, Mary Lou Malzone, Tom Martin, Jennifer Petersen, Janice Potts, Jessica Price, Jeanne Datz Rice, Tom Riford, Meredith Rufino, Peter Slavin, Carlyle Fairfax Smith, Gary Stephenson, Ruth E. Thaler-Carter, Elaine Mudrick Tom, Steve Trombetti, Beverly Westcott, Carolyn Wilks, Robert Williams, and Connie Yingling.

She thanks the Maryland Office of Tourism and all the wonderful people who took the time to assist her in researching *It Happened in Maryland.*

INTRODUCTION

If you picked up this book, you probably already know that Maryland is a dynamic, unique state. What you may not know is some of its fascinating history. The nation's seventh state may be small in size, but its people and history are anything but minor. Many events and notable people over the state's nearly four hundred–year history have shaped the country and even the world.

For example, techniques that dramatically changed the way we treat battlefield injuries to this day—and that have saved thousands of lives—were first implemented in Maryland during the Civil War. The predecessor to the nation's current interstate highway system originated in the state—in the 1800s, long before automobiles. And the state played an integral part in the Underground Railroad, Prohibition, and even the civil rights movement.

One piece of history that originated in Maryland has affected almost every American citizen, and is particularly dear to me. It all began with small, seemingly harmless turtles . . .

Prior to the 1970s, you could buy a cute little turtle for a dime or a quarter at a circus or a five-and-dime store. While I was a legislative aide to Prince George's County Councilman Francis B. Francois in the 70s, these little critters came to my attention. They had earned a horrible reputation, as they were bred in human waste and subsequently were spreading salmonella. The dangers were obvious: salmonella can be fatal to infants and senior citizens, and can wreak scatological havoc on your household pet if it drinks any of the water in the turtle bowl. The hazards were too many, so the sale of these turtles could not continue.

INTRODUCTION

After extensive research and documentation, Frank took up my turtle-ban mission and submitted a bill that would prohibit their sale within the county boundaries. It was adopted, and on the day the bill was signed, I was presented with a turtle pull toy. I was, from then on, officially dubbed the "turtle lady". My young daughters tried to buy a turtle at the local pet store to celebrate (or test) the bill's enactment, and they were told that some lady in Upper Marlboro had made it impossible for him to sell them.

Whenever someone felt the need or desire to give me a gift, it was a little turtle. I treasured these mementos made of china, wood, clay, seashells, cloth, silver, and a dizzying array of other materials. I finally stopped counting when my collection reached a hundred.

Within four years of the passing of the turtle bill, the federal government made the ban effective nationwide. The prohibition that started in Prince George's County made ripples throughout the nation. This event, along with countless other things small and large, makes Maryland so very one-of-a-kind.

GOOD THINGS COME IN
SMALL PACKAGES

In the seventeenth century, geographical boundaries in the American colonies were decided, as were many things, by people (e.g., kings) who lived an ocean away and had little understanding of the size and scope of this continent. Many Europeans still have this trouble and in a visit over our Fourth of July holiday will want to go to both Niagara Falls and Disney World by car and without reservations. "They look so close on the map," they say.

King Charles I issued a royal charter in 1632 creating Maryland as a place for Catholics to dwell without religious harassment. The original northern border was at 40 degrees north latitude, which was fine except it cut into the city of Philadelphia and the government of Pennsylvania wasn't going to let that happen.

As with many borders and boundaries, access to navigable water was a major issue. In this case, Maryland and Pennsylvania disagreed over access to the Delaware River and Delaware Bay, which empties into the Atlantic Ocean at Cape Henlopen. Pennsylvania wanted river frontage to avoid having to contend with Maryland to access the ocean. And, of course, Pennsylvania's leaders were already upset about Maryland's infringement into Philadelphia. Additionally, having more land would bring more settlers who farmed and created business enterprises that could be taxed to support the colony. If Pennsylvania had more land, Maryland would have less.

In 1682 the issue was temporarily decided when the monarchy allowed Pennsylvania to rent those lands of Delaware within a twelve-mile radius of the church at New Castle and all other lands south of that arc to Cape Henlopen. Maryland contested this decision, so King Charles II gave it to the Committee for Trade and Plantations, which decided that year that Delaware should be a separate jurisdiction. The debate continued for another fifty years. By 1732 Lord Baltimore had reached an understanding with Pennsylvania (and Delaware) on the location of Maryland's eastern border in exchange for relocating its northern border to be fifteen miles south of Philadelphia's South Street, or 39° 43' North. Lord Baltimore was perplexed about their easy agreement until he realized that his map put Cape Henlopen in Fenwick Island, about twenty-five miles south of the cape's actual location.

Representatives started discussing the border movement. All was going well—except the residents of Delaware were mostly Protestants and were concerned about their existence should the predominantly Catholic Maryland take over their territory.

Discussions would continue for decades as Maryland argued what it thought its proper borders should be, but to no avail. This is where Charles Mason and Jeremiah Dixon, preeminent scientists, came into the picture. In 1763 they began surveying the border. It took them five years to measure and survey the radius of northern Delaware, the transpeninsular line that ran north and south (halfway between the Atlantic and Chesapeake Bay), and the line that defined the border between Pennsylvania and Maryland.

To fix the boundaries, they placed a simple twelve-inch square stone marker every mile with a "P" on the Pennsylvania side and an "M" on the Maryland side. A more elaborate stone, with Lord Baltimore's coat of arms on the Maryland side and the Penn family crest on the Pennsylvania side, was placed every five miles. In all, they positioned more than two hundred stones that had come by ship from Portland, in southern England, and then by wagon. They set the stones as far as Sideling Hill (Washington County) and then left the rest at Fort Frederick because the terrain was too difficult to navigate with the weight of the stones.

Beyond Fort Frederick, they built earthen mounds about ten to fifteen feet in diameter and used a wooden post or built a stone mound to mark the boundary. Most have been inventoried since the turn of this century and ten are destroyed or missing.

One little border wedge remained a no-man's or every-man's land, for it lay between the 39° 43' mark, the Twelve-Mile Circle and Maryland's northern border. It took the states' government until 1921 to decide that this piece of property, barely over one square mile, belonged to Delaware with the north mark determined as an extension of the east–west portion of the Mason-Dixon Line, on the west by the north–south portion of the line, and on the southeast by the New Castle Twelve-Mile Circle.

The battle over what is now the two southern counties on the Eastern Shore that belong to Virginia also was based in religion. Protestant Virginians had settled in those lands and, again, they did not want to be under Catholic rule. Charles I agreed and changed the line so the southern portion of the peninsula started at Watkin's Point and ran due east to the Atlantic. More measuring blunders occurred, Watkin's Point was swallowed by the bay, and the line ran uphill rather than due east. After years of protest by Maryland, ignored because of more pressing political matters, a commission finally considered the border issue and in 1877 decided the border should stay where it was.

Meanwhile, the southern border between Maryland and Virginia on the western side of the Chesapeake Bay was defined by the Potomac River, a natural dividing line. However, the river's source was unknown, as was the fact that it had two branches. Once the fork or confluence was discovered, about eight miles southeast of Cumberland, Maryland claimed the southern branch and Virginia (this was before West Virginia broke away) claimed its land ran to the northern branch. As the older colony, Virginia's claim held, once again depriving Maryland of additional lands. Maryland's western border was then determined by a line going due north from the headwaters of the Potomac's northern branch to the Pennsylvania border.

As if Maryland hadn't suffered enough shrinkage, President George Washington received permission from Congress in 1790 to find one hundred square miles along the Potomac River to create the new capital city. As there were active ports in Alexandria in Virginia and Georgetown in Maryland, the sides of the square were slanted to include them. Additionally, the eastern branch of the Potomac, or what is now the Anacostia River, was easily navigable up to Bladensburg (where the British landed in 1814 when they attacked and burned Washington). Washington selected a point about five miles up the Anacostia (about where Robert F. Kennedy stadium is now) for the northeast border and a point about three miles up the Potomac for the northwest border.

So, starting in 1682 and continuing through the early 1900s, the lands within Maryland's original borders were relentlessly nibbled away from Maryland's northern, eastern, and southern boundaries like a pack of mice chewing at a piece of cheese. Thus, when you look at a list of states by size, Maryland is ninth smallest (after Rhode Island, Delaware, Connecticut, Hawaii, New Jersey, Massachusetts,

New Hampshire, and Vermont). At 9,775 square miles of land (not including the Chesapeake Bay and its tributaries), the state is larger than Vermont by 534 square miles, but the next largest is West Virginia at a whopping 24,087 square miles. We just have to be happy that good things come in small packages.

REPUDIATION DAY

Located in the deep recesses of most American brains are vague recollections from high school history classes about the Stamp Act, the Boston Tea Party, and an eight-year battle called the American Revolution (1775–1783). Depending on your love of history, you may know more details and even dates, but a few things did and did not happen that might make you say, "I didn't know that."

England and France had been battling each other in what was called the Seven Years' War unless you lived in the colonies, where it was called the French and Indian Wars (1754–1763, and yes, that's more than seven years, but that's another part of history). At war's end, the victor, Britain, controlled all of America from the Atlantic Ocean to the Mississippi River, as well as most of Canada.

To help recoup the monies spent on the wars and the annual cost of providing personnel to protect and preserve the colonies, the British Parliament enacted the Stamp Act on March 22, 1765. Their thinking was that if they were going to defend the new country, then we should be willing to pay for that defense. The act went into effect on November 1, 1765, and levied a tax on an assortment of paper products including bills, bonds, deeds, insurance policies, lawyers' licenses, leases, liquor permits, newspapers, pamphlets, playing cards, school diplomas, and wills, which covered pretty much everything written in daily life. Oh, and on dice, too. Each item required a stamp to prove the tax had been paid. The tax on printed matter, such as newspapers and pamphlets, was determined by the number of pages and advertisements.

Ranging from a half penny to ten pounds, these taxes were already in effect in Great Britain, and the Parliament figured that we'd be so pleased they had defeated the French that we'd be delighted to help repay them for their efforts. No, they didn't ask us whether this would delight us or whether it would cause a hardship on our daily existence.

Our coffers weren't too flush and the price of tobacco (a primary cash crop) had dropped precipitously, adding to a depressed economy. The taxes most definitely affected the powerful and vocal, including attorneys, barkeeps, and most important, printers, who could publish papers and pamphlets designed to incite the local residents. It was one thing to pay import or customs fees on items made in England. It was another to pay on products that were produced and used here. The consensus was that only locally elected governmental bodies could impose local taxes. To emphasize this point, the colonists refused to import goods from Great Britain.

Marylanders received the news of the tax in the April 18, 1765, issue of the *Maryland Gazette*, published by Jonas Green, who posted the notice and continued to do so every week for the next few months. By August 22, an Annapolitan, Zachariah Hood, had been named to the position of stamp distributor and collector. Fortunately for Hood, he was in Great Britain when the announcement reached Maryland. Four days after his appointment was made public, effigies of Hood were carried throughout Frederick, Baltimore, and

Annapolis, and his home was burned. When he returned, he had to sneak off the ship and then travel to New York for British protection.

On November 23, 1765, the twelve judges of the Frederick County Court—Joseph Smith, David Lynn, Charles Jones, Samuel Beall, Joseph Beall, Peter Bainbridge, Thomas Price, Andrew Hough, William Blair, William Luckett, James Dickson, and Thomas Beatty—the county's governing body, decided that the county's businesspeople did not have to comply with the Stamp Act, saying, "It is the unanimous resolution and opinion of this court that all business thereof shall and ought to be transacted in the usual and accustomed manner." They continued with, "And, that all proceedings shall be valid and effective without the use of stamps."

At the time, Frederick County encompassed today's Frederick County and the rest of western Maryland. Thus, this was the first body to officially oppose the tax. The Maryland Provincial Assembly soon followed. A week later the Sons of Liberty of Frederick County held a mock funeral of the despised edict. Eventually the other colonies followed suit in opposing the tax.

Although few may remember now, November 23 became known as Repudiation Day and for decades was celebrated as a half-day holiday where businesses, banks, schools, and others would close at noon. Today the local chapter of the Daughters of the American Revolution meet and the clerk of the circuit court reads the original declaration.

Even British merchants were up in arms by then because the colonists were refusing to buy goods made in Great Britain. Boycotting tea was one matter; boycotting every import was another. By March 18, 1766, with the writing on the wall, Parliament repealed the Stamp Act, effective May 1, 1766. They also enacted the Declaratory Act, which said they still had the authority to pass any legislation they wanted to regarding the colonies.

Deterred but not dissuaded, the British imposed the Townshend Acts, which decreed the governors and judges of the colonies were independent of colonial control. British troops were sent to Boston in 1768 and were met with great objection. Taxation without representation was more than the saying on a future bumper sticker.

Finally the dear people of Boston had had enough and on December 16, 1773, they boarded three ships filled with tea and dumped the goods into the harbor.

Fast-forward a few months to May 23, 1774, to Chestertown on Maryland's Eastern Shore and the local residents had what appeared to be their own version of a tea party, supposedly dumping a load of tea off the brigantine *Geddes* into the Chester River. This apocryphal tale has been handed down for the better part of two centuries and makes for a great annual gathering of several thousand people over Memorial Day weekend with a parade, crafts fair, music, and the symbolic tossing of tea and men into the river. Sorry—according to Adam Goodheart's research, it didn't happen. Serving on the editorial board of Phi Beta Kappa's *The American Scholar* magazine from 1998 to 2003, Goodheart and Erin Koster (a junior at the school at the time) delved into the past to determine the exact events of the Maryland town's tea party and came up with nothing.

A decade would pass between the decision by the Frederick judges and the time the war started at Lexington, Massachusetts, but the idea of a revolution had been formed in Frederick and was snowballing its way into an avalanche known as "the shot heard 'round the world."

In 1965 then–US representative Charles "Mac" Mathias (1922–2010) of Maryland's Sixth Congressional District, said, "This truly was one of the preambles of the American Revolution. It is an act we should remember. . . . For more important than that it set the stage for the Revolution was the fact that these judges illustrated the power and importance of an independent and courageous judiciary."

THE ROAD THAT BUILT THE NATION

1806

Long before President Dwight D. Eisenhower called for a national interstate road system and the Federal-Aid Highway Act of 1956 was approved to construct it, George Washington called for a highway that would connect the states on the Atlantic Ocean side of the country to the Ohio River and beyond. It took until 1806 for the US Congress and President Thomas Jefferson to authorize money to build the National Road (sometimes called the National Pike), the first federally funded and constructed road. It started in Cumberland, Maryland, at the end of navigable Potomac River waters and went to the Ohio River at Wheeling, West Virginia (which was then part of Virginia).

In Frederick the National Road crossed several north–south roads that led up and down the valley to Pennsylvania and Virginia. A historic National Road marker notes that Kimball's Inn, Talbott's Tavern, the City Hotel, and the Francis Scott Key Hotel were busy providing a "good night's rest" for tired travelers. Just as the settlers trod this path, so have presidential motorcades going to Camp David in the Catoctin Mountains north of town. Admittedly, they usually fly in by helicopter these days, but in the past they arrived by car.

Hancock, located at the narrowest section of Maryland measured north to south, is where you turn north to travel along what is now Interstate 70 to Pennsylvania or stay west to ride along Interstate 68. In either case, you bypass the town that was a busy stop along the National Road. There travelers would load up on provisions before tackling the mountains on the way to Cumberland or rest after the arduous trek from Cumberland. The town was filled with inns and hotels and places to eat and tend to horses and other livestock.

Over the next few years, segments were added in each direction, with pieces from Baltimore to Cumberland, through Hagerstown, Hancock, and Frostburg, finished by 1824 and then as far west as the Kaskaskia River in Vandalia, Illinois, by 1838, when Congress stopped approving more money. From Wheeling, the road followed Zane's Trace to Zanesville, Ohio (both of which were named for Colonel Ebenezer Zane, who constructed the route).

The 620-mile connection (which eventually provided the backbone for Route 40) between the Potomac and Ohio Rivers provided an easy gateway for thousands of pioneers. Near Grantsville, Maryland, the Casselman River Bridge was the world's longest single-span stone arch bridge at the time and the nearby Casselman Inn served passengers from as many as forty wagons a day. Several original milestones remain along Route 40, Alternate Route 40, and Scenic Route 40. You also can find mile markers in some places that state the distance to the next city or town, going east and west. Generally they are four-sided pyramid shapes with a capstone, and although they look like white stone, they are made of metal.

The pioneers of this road traveled by stagecoach, Conestoga wagon (also called the ship of inland commerce), and horseback, and some by foot, stopping at numerous towns and way stations at stagecoach inns—sometimes several to a town. In some areas where the road was rough or mountainous and travelers didn't make many miles in a day, the inns were as close as a mile apart. In other areas where the wagons could cover greater distances in the daylight hours or for as long as a horse team could last before being changed, the inns might be eight or even fifteen miles apart. As most people were going west, these inns were almost always on the northern side of the road.

Remnants of the old road remain, sometimes with physical buildings and sometimes only with markers. Toll houses were erected once the individual states took over responsibility for maintenance from the federal government. You can see the old two-story, seven-sided brick toll house in La Vale, Maryland, complete with accommodations for the toll keeper and his family and a chart listing the prices for passage. Tolls ranged from one cent for a mile to fifty-six cents for a score of cattle traveling thirty-five miles and eighty-eight cents for a carriage with four horses going thirty-five miles. The government determined the tolls according to how much damage they thought different sizes and weights of vehicles and animals would cause, collecting almost $10,000 in the first year at La Vale.

It took until 1818 for the 132-mile segment of highway to be completed, passing through twenty miles of Garrett County before heading north to Pennsylvania and west to Wheeling. It roughly followed an earlier track, the Braddock Road that ran between Cumberland and the Ohio River at Pittsburgh, but changed direction around Uniontown, Pennsylvania, to take a more southern route to Wheeling.

Almost one hundred years later, in 1912 the road became part of the National Old Trails Road connecting New York City to San Francisco. In 1928 and 1929, twelve statues honoring the pioneer woman were created by sculptor August Leimbach (1882–1965) of

St. Louis. The first geographically, although the last to be dedicated, is one in Bethesda, Maryland. Five are located on the National Trail: at Beallsville, Pennsylvania; Wheeling, West Virginia; Springfield, Ohio; Richmond, Indiana; and Vandalia, Illinois. The statues then follow the old Route 66 for a while, eventually ending at Upland, California.

The original Potomac River route of the National Road to Cumberland bypassed Washington County's Sideling Hill, an obstacle that later caused Interstate 70 heading west from Baltimore and Washington, D.C., to turn north from Hancock to Breezewood, Pennsylvania. Following the natural slope of the mountain would have produced a grade too steep for tractor trailers hauling heavy loads. It took more than a dozen years to cut through Sideling and create Interstate 68. Fortunately, or unfortunately, it connects only to Morgantown, West Virginia. It does provide a Pennsylvania Turnpike bypass by connecting to Interstate 79 heading north/south to Buffalo, New York, and the Canadian border.

The Sideling Hill cut, however, exposed a syncline created when the mountains were formed about 230 million to 345 million years ago and is a spectacular sight. Among the notable mile and historical markers are those for Negro Mountain, which at 2,940 feet is the highest point on the road. The mountain is named for Nemesis, a black frontiersman who was killed in battle while fighting with Thomas Cresap in the 1750s against local Native Americans. (A skirmish arose in 2011, not for the first time, when a Maryland state senator introduced legislation to rename Negro and Polish Mountains due to "cultural sensitivities." After protests from citizens and elected officials from the area, the measure was defeated.)

The plans to continue the road to St. Louis on the Mississippi River and then on to Jefferson City, Missouri, were dropped. Besides the financial issue of building the road, the Baltimore and Ohio

Railroad, which also connected Baltimore to Wheeling, was expanding westward and increasing in popularity as a faster way to travel than by wagon.

Once completed, the National Road that was started in 1806 allowed adventuresome people to travel beyond the eastern part of the country, following the advice offered by John B. L. Soule and popularized by Horace Greeley to "Go West, young man, go West and grow up with the country."

BATTLE OF BALTIMORE
(FORT MCHENRY)

Explaining what didn't happen at the Battle of Baltimore, also known as the battle at Fort McHenry (September 12–14, 1814), should come before the explanation of what did happen.

Francis Scott Key was not a prisoner of war.

Betsy Ross did not make the huge flag that flew over the fort.

It was a critical decisive moment in the War of 1812 or it was barely a skirmish (take your pick). Even the National Park Service says the battle was "one of its most obscure conflicts."

Mr. Peabody and Sherman may not have ventured to Fort McHenry with the WABAC (wayback) machine during *The Rocky and Bullwinkle Show* in the 1960s.

Even "authorities" have differing opinions about this battle, so we'll rely on the narrative told at the fort, which is a National Monument and Historic Shrine operated by the National Park Service.

By the early 1800s Baltimore was a thriving port city with many of its almost fifty thousand residents involved in shipbuilding and trade that connected areas north, south, and west of the city with the rest of the world.

Parts of the rest of the world, particularly France and Great Britain, were battling each other and the British were attacking and commandeering our freight-carrying ships and the crew, forcing them into service with the Royal British Navy. The pay was bad and the living conditions were worse. Additionally, many Americans felt the British were siding with the Indians to attack settlers trying to establish communities in the western part of our country.

Tempers flared on this side of the Atlantic and on June 18, 1812 (while the British were still busy fighting the Napoleonic Wars), we declared war against Britain, and our ship owners started capturing British ships. The British thought Baltimore was a "nest of pirates"; thus, we figured Baltimore probably was going to be attacked. Over the next several months the defenses at Fort McHenry, originally constructed between 1799 and 1802, were improved. Eventually a fleet of merchant ships were sunk in the harbor to create a blockade that would prevent enemy penetration.

One aspect of the preparation was the creation of a suitable flag. Fort personnel relate the tale that Major George Armistead, the commanding officer, wanted "to have a flag so large that the British will have no difficulty in seeing it from a distance."

Two flags were ordered from Mary Pickersgill, an esteemed Baltimore flag maker. One was to be the largest garrison flag ever (measuring thirty feet by forty-two feet) and the other a smaller (seventeen feet by twenty-five feet) storm flag. Within six weeks, with the help of her daughter and niece, the woolen flags were finished. Each had fifteen stars and fifteen stripes, one for each state in the union.

Led by Major General Robert Ross, the British sailed from Bermuda's Royal Naval Dockyard in August 1814, easily defeating our armies at the Battle of Bladensburg on August 24, then proceeding toward Washington, D.C. Our military was long gone from Washington, so the British were free to loot and burn the public buildings, including the White House, Capitol, Library of Congress, Washington Navy Yard, and other government buildings. After plundering valuables from the city, the British headed toward Baltimore in a two-pronged attack.

Under Ross's command, the British attacked by land at North Point with five thousand soldiers, with General John Stricker leading three thousand men in defense of the city. Ross was killed by a sharpshooter early in the battle, placing Colonel Arthur Brooke in command. He was not nearly the battle-savvy leader Ross had been and he decided to wait until the battle at Fort McHenry was over rather than continue the march into the city. In other words, we retreated, but Brooke didn't pursue our fleeing army. We didn't lose, but the British didn't win.

The White House asked Francis Scott Key, a prominent thirty-four-year-old Washington, D.C., attorney and amateur poet, to negotiate for the release of the elderly mayor of Upper Marlboro, Dr. William Beanes, who had put British soldiers in jail because they were drunk and mean to the townspeople. Key had letters of high praise for the doctor written by wounded British officers, commending his ability and concern for them as his patients. His release was granted. However, the Brits, after Key had dined on the admiral's ship, told him he had to wait there lest he tell the Marylanders the British were about to strike.

Vice Admiral Sir Alexander Cochrane coordinated the naval attack on the fort with nineteen ships, resulting in firepower that was much stronger than the guns at Fort McHenry. The sunken-ship blockade worked and the British ships were pulled back so they would be out of range of the fort's cannons, where one thousand soldiers defended the fort and the city.

According to the Park Service, the British threw bombs, rockets, and another weapon called a *carcass,* a hollow cast-iron spherical shell that weighed 190 pounds and differed from the exploding bombs in that it set buildings on fire, at the fort. The projectile also proved useful at night, because it burned for eleven minutes after firing and it helped aim other shells. Instead of one vent hole for a single fuse, the carcass had three openings, each two inches in diameter, and was filled with an incendiary composition.

Dozens of ten- and thirteen-inch shells and four carcasses were thrown toward the fort by the HMS *Volcano,* which was only one of the ships in the Patapsco River. It's thought that the majority of the carcasses were saved to throw at the city to set it on fire.

For twenty-five hours the British continued the bombardment, and on the morning of September 14 the storm flag was lowered and the oversize flag was raised over the fort, inspiring Key to pen the "Defence of Fort McHenry" poem, with these opening lines:

O say, can you see, by the dawn's early light,
What so proudly we hailed at the twilight's last gleaming?

Today the oversize flag is on display at the Smithsonian Institution's National Museum of American History in Washington, D.C.

Although not defeated at Fort McHenry, the British certainly weren't victorious, and the naval and land soldiers left for New Orleans.

Robert Devaney, executive director of the Francis Scott Key Foundation in Washington, D.C., says, "The battle was huge for the USA. The British navy was finally stopped after a year of sailing around the Chesapeake freely. While the battles on Lake Erie and at the frontier were perhaps more important, the Brits could have split the young nation in half at Baltimore, after having burned its little capital—news of which resulted in bad public relations for the empire throughout the cities of Europe.

"The song certainly heightened the import of this battle—but it is more important to note that it perfectly articulated our young country's acceptance of themselves and the world as 'Americans.' The anthem taps into an awakening of a new national mindset: We are all Americans now.

"Like Russia during this time, America had survived an invasion from a European superpower—and both began their own march to becoming superpowers."

On March 3, 1931, Congress, with President Herbert Hoover, made the "Star-Spangled Banner" the national anthem.

BLADENSBURG DUELING GROUND

1839

Dueling probably started at least during medieval times. Or maybe it's older than recorded history, when one caveman thought another was poaching on the animal the first man had slain. Who knows what those cave drawings mean?

By the time men had hand coverings, one man would throw a gauntlet (glove) to the ground to challenge a second man to a duel in response to an insult the second had placed upon the first—thus the expression "throwing down the gauntlet." Men could and would battle over a woman's reputation, parentage, land ownership, and many other issues. Swords or pistols were drawn and the better swordsman or marksman usually won, regardless of whom or what the challenge represented. Records exist of duels in Europe, Asia, South America, and, of course, North America.

A Code Duello was adopted in 1777 Ireland that prescribed the rules and dictated that such battles were to be "conducted coolly, courteously, and steadily." It defined how distances were to be set, the selection of weapons, and the necessity of seconds (representatives) to defend the duelers' honor. The seconds were called into play should one of the duelers shoot before the count of one or after the count of three.

The practice of settling a dispute came to this continent with the Europeans, though they primarily fought duels with pistols here rather than with swords. Fine gentlemen would own an equally matched set of exquisite dueling pistols as befit his rank in society. Modern filmmakers have extolled the workmanship of dueling pistols where the pair are presented to the person being challenged to pick which gun he wants to use, thus theoretically giving both men guns of equal capabilities.

More than four dozen duels were held on the Bladensburg Dueling Ground, one of the most famous of all such places. It was situated along the Eastern Branch of the Anacostia River (formerly Dueling Creek), just over the border between Maryland and Washington, D.C. Starting as early as 1808, many of the combatants were residents of Washington, D.C., where the practice was illegal. It was also illegal in Maryland, but Maryland laws did not apply to Washington residents even for actions that took place in Maryland. The dueling ground now is a little park with a sign denoting its place in history.

In today's light (and maybe then, too), the reasons for a duel might seem ridiculous, including one that supposedly was fought over how fast a steamboat was traveling. Others were more serious.

Two of the most infamous battles in America were between Alexander Hamilton (former secretary of the treasury) and Aaron Burr (vice president of the United States) on July 11, 1804, which Hamilton did not survive, and between Andrew Jackson (who would become the seventh president) and Charles Dickinson (a well-known duelist who did not survive this battle). The Hamilton-Burr contest stirred the nation's disapproval of dueling but did not squelch it.

Dueling began to decline around the Revolutionary War. George Washington did not want his officers competing to protect their own honor when they had so much to protect against the British military. As most officers were highly trained in hand-to-hand combat, whether by sword or by pistol, any loss of life to a duel cost the country an officer in the war. Additionally, average citizens saw the cost of battle in the numbers of sons, husbands, and relatives killed and thought there had to be a better way to resolve a slight or misunderstanding than taking another man's life.

One duel was fueled by a naval incident in 1807. At that time Captain James Barron was ordered to sail an American warship, USS *Chesapeake,* to the Mediterranean Sea. A British ship officer demanded that Barron turn over some Americans the British claimed had deserted from the British navy. Barron refused, and the English fired, killing three men and wounding eight more, and then took possession of the alleged deserters. Barron was tried and suspended from duty.

During his naval career and short life Commodore Stephen Decatur Jr. had proven himself as an extraordinary naval officer and hero. He built the three-story home now known as the Decatur House on Lafayette Square, across from the White House in Washington, D.C., where he and his wife were involved in the city's social life while he worked at the Navy Department.

Between Barron's court-martial hearing and the War of 1812, Barron and Decatur exchanged numerous letters, each more derogatory and insulting than the one before. With the onset of the war, Barron tried to reenter the Navy and Decatur opposed his reappointment. Decatur, who had sat on the Barron court-martial trial board and was now on the board that approved such appointments, was particularly opposed to the reappointment. Barron challenged Decatur to a duel.

Unfortunately, Decatur asked Commodore William Bainbridge to be his second, thinking the man was a friend. He wasn't and

Bainbridge agreed to dueling conditions that were not conducive to Decatur's survival. It would take thirteen years from insult to death, but Barron finally won his revenge on March 20, 1820.

In another prominent incident, Daniel Key, eldest son of Francis Scott Key, was killed in a duel against John F. Sherburne, both midshipmen at the US Naval Academy. According to Robert Devaney, executive director of the Francis Scott Key Foundation in Washington, D.C. Daniel was nineteen at the time of the battle in mid-June 1836.

It took a duel on February 24, 1838, between the popular Congressman Jonathan Cilley of Maine and Congressman William J. Graves of Kentucky (substituting for James W. Webb, editor of the *New York Courier* and *Enquirer* newspaper and a strong Graves political supporter), to finally get stronger laws against dueling. Webb had written that Cilley was corrupt, and Cilley took offense and challenged him to a duel. Unfortunately for Cilley, Webb's second, Graves, was an excellent marksman. Although Cilley used a rifle and they exchanged three shots before anyone was hit, Graves's third shot pierced Cilley's femoral artery and he bled to death in less than two minutes.

Almost a year later to the day, on February 20, 1839, Congress strengthened the rules against dueling in Washington to include challenging someone to a duel or even accepting a challenge to duel. However, men of honor continued to challenge each other in secret and the duels were scheduled to start before the sun had risen or as it was setting, making the legislation ineffective.

Despite various states and other foreign countries denouncing dueling, it was well after the American Civil War before the practice was officially prohibited in the United States and its popularity had died, much as so many had done on the field of honor. Reportedly the last duel ever held was in France in 1967: Gaston Deferre and René Ribière used swords, with Deferre being victorious. Fortunately, neither man died.

UNDERGROUND RAILROAD

1835

Should you explore the nineteenth-century phenomenon known as the Underground Railroad, you'll run into lots of stories, most of them anecdotal and perhaps some debatable. The Underground Railroad started in its prime in 1831. It was neither underground nor a railroad that ran on tracks. Travel happened at night and everything involved was a secret (ergo, the term "underground," as was later used by spies during World War II) association of brave people, both white and black, who helped slaves escape from the Southern states. The people who led them from place to place were called conductors or engineers. The places where they stopped for food, shelter, and clothing were called stations, and those who owned the homes or businesses were station masters. Those escaping were called passengers, cargo, or goods.

Proof of these actions often is hard to come by because many of the people involved in helping slaves escape to Delaware on their way to the free North and Canada were compartmentalized. All they knew was who contacted them and whom they contacted. Helping to free slaves or even helping freed slaves travel north was a crime. So, for the same reason, few notes or records were kept. As any fan of police procedural books, television shows, and movies and of real life knows, you can't follow a paper trail if it isn't there. Fortunately, some notes and diaries were kept, particularly by people north of the Mason-Dixon Line, where slavery was illegal, so we can begin to understand what they went through and why. Runaway and freed slaves headed to Canada in particular, because slavery had been abolished there in 1834.

From this time and place comes the story of Harriet Tubman. Born a slave in 1822 in Bucktown, near Cambridge, Harriet committed her first reported act of defiance in the area where the Bucktown Village Store is located, sometime around 1835. She was helping a slave to freedom when she was hit in the head by the slave owner, which led to lifelong health problems and seizures. As a teenager she was hired out to John T. Stewart, who owned several farms, a shipyard, and other businesses. While there she met and married a freed slave, John Tubman, in 1844. Bucktown is where Tubman most likely learned the secret codes black mariners used and learned about safe places to live in the North.

Tubman escaped on September 17, 1849, and returned to help others escape. Making thirteen trips over the next decade, she helped an estimated seventy slaves—family members and friends—reach freedom. Providing assistance along the way were Jacob, Arthur, and Hannah Leverton (white Quakers whose brick home was known to be a major stopover), Daniel Hubbard (a free black ship carpenter), James Webb (whose log cabin can be seen on the 125-mile Underground Railroad trail), and Hugh Hazlett (who was captured and held in the Caroline County Courthouse in Denton for helping with the Railroad).

Samuel Green, a free black farmer and Methodist preacher, also was suspected of helping runaways. He was sentenced to ten years in prison at the Dorchester County Courthouse in Cambridge because he owned a copy of *Uncle Tom's Cabin,* the antislavery book written by Harriet Beecher Stowe in 1852. The courthouse that sits at 206 High Street was built in 1854, replacing the one that burned in 1852.

In addition to the people who ensured slaves' passage on the Railroad, some say songs helped to signal danger or a safe conduit. Such songs and spirituals as "Steal Away" and "Follow the Drinking Gourd" supposedly explained travel plans. The "drinking gourd" referred to the stars on the bottom of the bowl of the Big Dipper constellation that point toward the North Star. Other references indicated the Railroad was the freedom train or the gospel train that would take them to the Promised Land, or freedom up north.

Quilt designs were another possible aid to slaves seeking freedom. Anecdotal information indicates that designs were incorporated that showed a safe home, direction, or route or provided food, much as hobos riding the rails during the Depression in the next century would signal a home that provided food or an opportunity to work for clothing, money, or a bed. According to quilt theorists, there were ten patterns sewn into quilts that could be placed on a fence or clothesline, or hanging from a tree branch, alone or in combination, meaning "be prepared," "leave tonight," or "stay put." Even if apocryphal, this account conveys the unity and fear that all felt during the operation of the Railroad.

These slaves were fleeing owners who did not want them to learn to read or write, in no small part because they were afraid the slaves would read about escapes or learn to forge papers to prove someone was a free person. It's said that on one trip when Tubman was helping others escape, she pretended to be reading a newspaper and although people were looking for her, they knew she couldn't read, so they ignored her.

Many routes to freedom were land based, but others were via boats because of the proximity to the seventy-mile-long Choptank River, the Chesapeake Bay, and the Atlantic Ocean. Many boat or ship pilots were black and would hide fugitives on their way north. However, blacks worked as sailors, so it wasn't unusual to see them on a ship, even those captained or piloted by white men. Trains were used, too, and Frederick Douglass (1818–1895) was one slave who escaped by train from Baltimore to New York carrying freedom papers he borrowed from a black sailor.

Another incident involved John Bowley, a free black ship carpenter. His wife (Harriet Tubman's niece) and her two daughters were scheduled to be sold on the auction block in front of the Dorchester County Courthouse in 1850. The three of them managed to escape and Bowley spirited them away by boat to Baltimore. There they met with Tubman, who helped them reach safety in Philadelphia.

In 1854, around Christmas Day, Tubman led her three brothers to freedom from the area of Poplar Neck, Maryland. The property was owned by Dr. Anthony C. Thompson, who had many free and enslaved black laborers working for him, including Tubman's father, Ben Ross. Both her parents were also involved in the Underground Railroad and after her brothers' escape, Tubman feared for her parents' lives, so she returned to help them escape, too. As Tubman became better known, her life was ever more threatened and she had to abandon her trips in 1860. However, she did not retire quietly. Instead she continued her humanitarian practices as an activist, Civil War spy and nurse, and suffragist.

Assisting escaping slaves was a particularly brave thing to do in Maryland, where slavery had been legalized as early as 1660. When the Cambridge area of the Eastern Shore was settled in the mid-seventeenth century by whites from England, slaves, and free blacks, many were involved in farming. The original crop, tobacco, required many hours to grow and a lot of manpower—work done by slaves.

As the records are so sketchy, it's difficult to know how many slaves were escorted through the Eastern Shore and routes through western Maryland and other locales. It's difficult to know the effect of one person, such as Tubman, on the activities of others. A low estimate of escapees hinges around one thousand slaves a year from Maryland and other Southern states to a total of as many as 100,000 men, women, and children over the lifetime of the Railroad. Although the absolute numbers may have been small by comparison to the slave population, the psychological effect was enormous.

Finally, in 1864 slaves in Maryland were freed and the Thirteenth Amendment to the US Constitution abolished slavery. In 1865 the Civil War ended, with many of the events leading up to that point happening in Maryland's Dorchester and Caroline Counties.

SEVEN FOOT KNOLL LIGHTHOUSE

1855

As Baltimore became an increasingly popular port for commercial and passenger ships, safe navigation of the Chesapeake Bay and its tributaries became more important. Starting in the 1600s more than 2,400 ships were lost off the coast of Delaware and in the Chesapeake Bay due to storms, poor visibility, and unmarked underwater dangers. Many of them were mere wooden shells almost waiting to be dashed and smashed upon rocky shores. A few also sank due to pirate raids, military conflicts, human error, and other causes. Who knows how many lives were lost within those hundreds of sunken vessels?

Lighthouses and markers became essential, replacing buoys and flares as the primary guides toward unharmed passage through the night, the fog, and the devilish acts of pirates who would move the flares to misdirect trusting captains.

The Chesapeake Bay was originally a river that was flooded by rising sea levels about ten thousand years ago, at the end of the last ice age, submerging the Susquehanna River. The ice sheet did not reach that far south, so the riverbed and bay were not carved out of land, as were the Finger Lakes of New York. The soft, muddy bottom of the bay caused a serious construction problem for sinking lighthouse piers and foundations. Thus, a new type of lighthouse was constructed here: the screw pile. Developed in Great Britain, a screw-pile house usually sat on one central and eight exterior iron pilings, or legs, flaring gently outward rather than parallel to one another and perpendicular to the land. This formed an octagonal base that was easy and relatively inexpensive to build. Generally an octagonal house, one-and-a-half stories tall, sat on the base and the light was above the house.

After seven years of requests for a light and allowing time to construct it, the first one built in the Maryland waters of the bay was at Seven Foot Knoll, a shallow shoal at the entrance to the Patapsco River, which led to the port of Baltimore. It was finally completed in late 1855, replacing the 1823 Bodkin Island light on the southern side of the river mouth. The original Seven Foot Knoll house was replaced in 1875 with a cylindrical structure made of iron, unlike its cousins that were made of wood.

The Seven Foot Knoll light stood forty feet above mean high water and had a foghorn in addition to a fourth-order Fresnel lens. The lantern, visible for twelve miles, was lit every night and extinguished each morning. Built by the Murray and Hazelhurst ironworks of Baltimore, the walls, beams, and other parts were fabricated at the foundry and then brought to the site and assembled at a cost of $27,000.

One concern about a Chesapeake Bay lighthouse was the possibility of a frozen bay, and indeed, in January 1884 and again in 1894 ice broke some of the iron piles. Thus, large amounts of riprap eventually were placed around the pilings to help protect them from future ice attacks.

Inside the lighthouse, though, the keeper had responsibilities beyond maintaining the light and the home. The obvious one, using the light and foghorn, alerted ship captains to the underwater dangers around them so they could steer clear of the perils. A second one, experienced only upon rare occasions, involved helping rescue ship personnel from hazardous situations.

Thomas Jefferson Steinheise was the last of the civilian light keepers at Seven Foot Knoll, serving from 1930 to 1941. He was born in 1878 in Leonardtown, Maryland, and started his career as a waterman and blacksmith. He joined the US Lighthouse Service as an assistant keeper of the Tangier Sound Lighthouse in Virginia on August 1, 1918, serving with his brother-in-law, who was the head keeper. Steinheise was promoted in February 1919 and made keeper of the Lower Cedar Point Lighthouse on the Potomac River but resigned eight months later for unexplained or at least unrecorded reasons. He rejoined the service in March 1927, working at the Ragged Point lighthouse on the Potomac, and transferred to the Seven Foot Knoll light on December 16, 1930. He and his family stayed there, with farm animals living under the light (brought indoors during a storm or high seas) during the summer and flowers and vegetables grown outdoors on the walkway around the light. They easily caught fish, which they consumed or traded with farmers for produce and livestock.

Nothing in Steinheise's background seems to have prepared him for his finest hour. The highlight of his career came during a nor'easter on August 21, 1933 (the same storm that created the Ocean City inlet cut). Sometime after midnight he and his son Earl heard the cries of seamen who had been forced to abandon their sinking tug, the *Point Breeze*. The engine on his twenty-one-foot motorboat wouldn't start, so Steinheise had to row into the dangerous waters with fifteen-foot waves and hurricane-force ninety-mile-per-hour winds. He pulled six of the fourteen seamen and the captain from the dangerous waters. One of the men died, but Steinheise was honored for his bravery with the Commerce Department's Silver Life Saving Medal—the highest civilian honor presented. This lifesaving aspect was one reason the Seven Foot Knoll light remained staffed for as long as it did.

The light was automated in 1948, ending the history of keepers living in the house. Four decades later it was replaced by a steel skeleton tower. The City of Baltimore claimed the light when it was declared surplus, and Empire Construction removed the 220-ton structure and barged it to Pier 5 in the Inner Harbor. It has been renovated and is now open to the public as part of the Baltimore Maritime Museum. A year later, on August 22, 1989, the lighthouse was listed on the National Register of Historic Places.

In all, about one hundred screw-pile lights were built in the bay, off the coast of the Carolinas, along the Gulf of Mexico, in Long Island Sound, and even in Lake Erie. Of those, forty-two were built in the bay and of those, only four still stand, including Seven Foot Knoll; the Thomas Point Shoal light (1875), originally located near the mouth of the South River and the only screw-pile light still in its original location; the Hooper Strait light (1879), originally at Tangier Sound and now forty miles away at the Chesapeake Bay Maritime Museum in St. Michaels (since 1966); and the Drum Point light (1883), which originally guarded the northern mouth of the Patuxent River and was moved to the Calvert Marine Museum in Solomons, becoming an exhibit in 1978.

Although a handful of lighthouses featured similar construction, none had the history or the longevity of the Seven Foot Knoll lighthouse.

BATTLEFIELD TRIAGE

1862

Without a doubt, the Civil War Battle of Antietam (frequently called the Battle of Sharpsburg by Southerners) on September 17, 1862, was a major event that had a great effect on the shaping of our state and country. According to Tom Riford, president and CEO of the Hagerstown-Washington County Convention and Visitors Bureau, The day of the battle was "America's single bloodiest," with 23,110 casualties (dead, wounded, or missing, including six generals who died in the battle), much more than any other one-day battle.

Although neither side had a decisive victory, President Abraham Lincoln finally had a sufficient enough triumph that he felt comfortable releasing the preliminary Emancipation Proclamation. This began the process of freeing the slaves and forever established that the war was about ending slavery. This also kept England and France from recognizing the Confederacy and participating in the war. Within two years, slavery in the United States was illegal.

Clara Barton's first battle was Antietam. This volunteer nurse became known as the "Angel of the Battlefield" and later would help establish and lead the American Red Cross.

Battlefield photography started at Antietam, with photos taken by Alexander Gardner (of Matthew Brady's studio) of the dead and also of battle damage.

It was the first major battle in the Civil War to take place on Northern soil.

The rolling hills, cornfields, woods, split rail–and–stone fences, limestone outcroppings, and other terrain provided excellent coverage and protection from an attacking army and excellent points from which to attack. Smokeless gunpowder hadn't been invented yet so visibility on the smoky fields was nearly zero, units marched shoulder to shoulder so each soldier knew the man standing next to him was friend, not foe. Additionally, most (if not all) weapons did not have rifled barrels, so the bullets and cannonballs were not propelled very far or with any great accuracy. To some extent, one army had to be almost on top of the opposition before any attack could be successful.

However, although the unharvested corn was about seven feet tall, the bayonets—another indication of nearly hand-to-hand combat—poised at rifle's end reflected the early morning sunlight and the soldiers were sitting ducks to the batteries of shells and canisters causing mass destruction and confusion. As the Union forces advanced, they cut the corn as close to the ground as possible and the bodies of soldiers fell in rows almost as neat as the cornstalks had been before the battle.

The month before, in August 1862, in the Second Battle of Manassas (Bull Run) in Virginia, many soldiers had died after being left on the battlefield for as long as a week, a common practice at the time. Injured soldiers died of thirst, hunger, exposure, infection, exsanguination, and similar causes. No one was appointed to remove the soldiers and bring them to a field hospital station. If they couldn't walk (or crawl or have a buddy help) to the hospital, they were basically abandoned.

Now, the battle at Antietam, which started in a foggy morning and progressed to a humid seventy-five degrees, was different from the one at Manassas. Besides the large number of wounded and killed, the primary difference was in how the injured soldiers were treated. At Antietam, thirty-eight-year-old Dr. Jonathan Letterman started the first systematic medical triage. As head of medical services for the Army of the Potomac, Letterman had seen how wounded soldiers had been treated in previous battles. Part of the new process implemented September 17, 1862, was making sure medical supplies were on hand and in sufficient quantity. Previously they had been allowed to dwindle or even been abandoned at the previous battle site.

Antietam also saw the start of the ambulance corps. Wagons carrying stretchers, lanterns, and other medical supplies were designated to pick up the wounded. Injured soldiers were placed on litters and carefully attended to rather than just stacked in a pile and left to bounce around as the wagons traveled rough and rutted roads. The ambulance drivers were military personnel under the command of a lieutenant, rather than civilians. In fact, many civilians were terrified of the battlefield and might have stayed around only long enough to pick the pockets of the injured and dead soldiers and to steal alcohol and medical supplies. They didn't always linger long enough to tend to the wounded.

Within twenty-four hours of the twelve-hour Antietam battle, all wounded were removed from the battlefield and taken to a field station, where they received an appraisal and initial treatment. Medical personnel separated the injured soldiers into those who would live with medical attention and those who wouldn't survive regardless of treatment. Those who needed additional treatment were sent to a field hospital—a barn, church, large house, or other large building—that had been commandeered in preparation for the battle, although sometimes only tents were set up in a field or thicket of trees. These buildings were chosen for their size and easy accessibility to and within the building. Another criterion was their location, which theoretically was away from the anticipated direction of the battle and far enough away to avoid having shells and gunshot aimed at them either intentionally or accidentally. A nearby supply of hay or straw, water, and food also figured into the hospital's location. These field hospitals would become today's MASH (mobile army surgical hospital) units.

The medical corps had an exaggeratedly negative reputation, with rumors of nearly barbaric treatment or lack of treatment. Often the family and friends of a wounded soldier would come to claim him and want to move him home. Prior to the triage system, men would have limbs amputated to avoid either infection or death from blood loss.

Each hospital was staffed with a head surgeon in charge of the facility, two assistant surgeons, six medical officers, hospital stewards, nurses, cooks, and other personnel. A chain of command was established to oversee the duties assigned to each member of the staff. Letterman also dictated and imposed strict sanitary regulations.

Additionally, Letterman made sure the doctors and medical personnel were drilled and tested on a regular basis to determine their medical understanding. They were then assigned to duties appropriate for their training, rather than their rank or length of service, as had previously been the case.

Seven months after Antietam, the ambulance corps and triage system had proven their worth again at the Battle of Gettysburg

(July 1–3, 1863) when 14,000 Union and 6,800 Confederate soldiers were wounded. The soldiers were removed quickly from the battlefield and taken to Camp Letterman, a medical facility about a mile out of Gettysburg. The location had been chosen because it bordered a main road and a railroad. Trains could provide supplies (medical and otherwise) to the camp and convey patients to larger medical facilities in Philadelphia, Baltimore, and Washington, D.C. The men were evaluated and treated and nearly 2,000 Union and 3,000 Confederate soldiers were considered to be too badly injured to survive a trip to a hospital; more than 370 of them died.

Tents were erected for dining, operating, and embalming, and for use as wards for the convalescing soldiers. Each of those ward tents had forty cots with mattresses and sheets. Archaeological digs have taken place in the Camp Letterman area, and licensed Gettysburg battlefield guide Phil Lechak notes that the camp also had a graveyard that has not yet been located.

Letterman died in 1872 at the age of forty-seven and was buried in Arlington National Cemetery. His gravestone calls him the man "who brought order and efficiency in to the Medical Service and who was the originator of modern methods of medical organization in armies." Nearly forty years after his death, the Army hospital at the Presidio in San Francisco was named in his honor. It's estimated that this triage system, which is still in effect, has saved thousands of lives by promptly removing wounded soldiers from the battlefield.

NIGHT SCHOOL

1878

America has been a land of immigrants since the Natives crossed the land bridge from Russia. Newcomers have traveled here in waves, escaping persecution, disease, and famine. As each wave moved up, another came in at the lowest rung, entering through ports in New York, Baltimore, Galveston, San Francisco, and other places. They brought their own traditions, foodstuffs, and language.

One particular wave took place in the late 1870s, and although family and friends could help newcomers find accommodations, meals, and employment, it was more difficult to fully assimilate into the community and to understand the area's broader practices and mores.

A Baltimore woman, Henrietta Szold (born in 1860), had been well educated and although she aspired to be a rabbi, that wasn't allowed in those days. Her father was the senior rabbi at Temple Oheb Shalom (Lover of Peace), the first conservative Jewish congregation in the United States. After moving from its original home near today's Oriole Park at Camden Yards in 1892 and then again in

1960, the synagogue moved to its current home in the Park Heights Avenue area in Pikesville.

The eldest of eight daughters (three died in infancy), Szold was a brilliant student who was graduated from Baltimore's Western Female High School in 1877 with high honors. Her father, teaching her as he would an eldest son, schooled her in Hebrew, German, and French. Her mother, Sophie Schaar Szold, taught her more domestic skills of sewing, cooking, and gardening.

In the 1870s Russian and Eastern European Jews were emigrating from their anti-Semitic societies to America, not knowing the first thing about daily life, so Szold started teaching English at night to help the immigrants understand their new country. On the first night, thirty-five people attended. The number doubled on the second night. Her students learned how to speak English, about history, how to deal with banks, where to shop for food and clothing, and all the other necessities of their new life.

Szold helped others in ways that would become events themselves, much as fire is not composed of atoms or matter, but is an event. Szold showed time after time that she was more of an event than a person. She accomplished other "firsts" that helped pave the way for those who followed her.

Barry Kessler, an independent historian and museum curator assembled a 1995 exhibit, "Daughter of Zion: Henrietta Szold and American Jewish Womanhood," for the Jewish Historical Society of Maryland. He notes that in 1902 Szold became the "first woman to enroll in the Jewish Theological Seminary (New York) saying she wanted to edit her late father's papers as a scholar and she needed the training" to do that. She was admitted with the provision that she not attempt to be ordained. Even though she agreed to that stipulation, "she blazed the trail for women rabbis," says Kessler.

In 1909, says Kessler, "A group of scholars and others raised money to send her to Palestine (now Israel), where she was inspired by the nurses who treated the diseased children." She was familiar with Settlement Houses in the United States, places where district nurses would go from one home or family to the next to perform minor medical projects, and she came up with the idea of bringing that practice to Jerusalem.

Realizing that women had little or no voice in men's organizations in a male-dominated world, she worked to create a women's organization. It took two years for her to put this idea into action, creating the Hadassah Women's Organization in Baltimore, and in 1912 she became its first national president. Today its 300,000 members make it the world's largest women's volunteer organization. The Hadassah Medical Center comprises two university hospitals in Jerusalem and medically related schools affiliated with the Hebrew University of Jerusalem. They continue to be funded, in large part, by Hadassah.

Although others might rest on the laurels of these accomplishments, Szold saw the rise of Adolf Hitler in the early 1930s, and when she was in her seventies (and living in Israel), she created a Youth Aliyah program to bring German Jewish children to agricultural settlements in Palestine. "Aliyah" can be interpreted to mean rising, ascent, or coming up, as in an ascent to Jerusalem or immigration into the country. This program expanded to other European countries and it's estimated that she saved thirty thousand children from Nazi-occupied Europe and Hitler's concentration camps.

Impressed with the work Szold was doing, Supreme Court Justice Louis Dembitz Brandeis (1856–1941) paid for her living expenses so she could work on a modern Jewish state. Brandeis was an active member of the Zionist movement, saying, "Every American Jew who aids in advancing the Jewish settlement in Palestine, though he feels that neither he nor his descendants will ever live there, will likewise be a better man and a better American for doing so."

Szold died on February 13, 1945, and was buried on the Mount of Olives in Jerusalem. The State of Israel issued a coin and a stamp honoring her, thus making her the first American and the first woman to be featured on Israeli currency. She died three years shy of seeing Israel become an independent state, thus winning the Zionist battle she had fought for throughout her adult life. Mother's Day, in Israel, is celebrated on the 30th of Shevat, the day Szold died in the Hebrew calendar.

Although she died more than sixty-five years ago, her work and dedication are alive today. The Henrietta Szold–Hadassah School of Nursing in Palestine, which had its first graduating class in 1921, is named for her and continues practicing her belief that all peoples, Jews and Arabs alike, should receive proper medical care and training.

Every chapter of Hadassah continues her work, and according to Dr. Emmanuel Grupper, director of the residential and guidance department and coordinator of the Youth Aliyah Friends Committee in Europe, orphaned and abandoned children are still being relocated to Israel in the Youth Aliyah program. In 2009, fifty-seven refugees were located in five youth villages.

With all her accomplishments, the medical breakthroughs that have been achieved, and the thousands of lives saved from persecution and death, perhaps the most lasting accomplishment was her first: the creation of night school programs. In 1888, ten years after Szold started it, her school was taken over by Baltimore City. By that time Szold had taught more than five thousand students and she had created the mold by which all future classes would be taught. Today thousands of foreign-born students are educated because of the night classes she started in 1878.

THE GREAT BALTIMORE FIRE

The Great Baltimore Fire of 1904 is almost always referred to as such. It's never just the "Baltimore Fire" or the "Great Fire." Yes, there were other Baltimore fires, notably in 1858 (proving the value of a steam fire engine with predictions that with enough such engines, Baltimore would never again suffer from large, city-wide fires) and in 1873, when 113 buildings were destroyed. Unfortunately, thirty-one years later the city still did not have enough equipment and this fire was monumental.

At 10:48 a.m. on a bitterly cold and windy winter Sunday morning in Baltimore, the first automatic fire alarm was sounded at the John E. Hurst & Company building. The six-story brick structure stood on the south side of German Street (now Redwood Street) between Hopkins Place and Liberty Street. Within its walls were the Hurst Company's stock of dry goods, cotton goods, and notions—perfect fuel for a fire. As the firefighters broke through the lower doors, the burst of fresh air created a backdraft and pushed the fire up the stairwell and elevator shaft.

Overwhelmed by the flames, the city firefighters sent telegraphs to nearby cities asking for help. The estimated forty-mile-per-hour winds fanned the blaze and the frigid weather tore at the firefighters. The blaze consumed block after block until it had destroyed more than 1,500 buildings in a seventy-block area.

More than 1,200 firefighters and members of the Maryland National Guard, Naval Brigade, and police officers from Baltimore and other jurisdictions battled the persistent flames and kept order in the city to avoid looting and injuries. Other fire companies rushed from forty-four cities and towns, including Washington, Philadelphia, Altoona, Annapolis, Chester, Harrisburg, Wilmington, York, Atlantic City, and as far away as New York.

In an attempt to create a firebreak, several buildings were dynamited, but that spread the conflagration rather than stopping it. The wind shifted a couple of times during the day, but it wasn't until around midnight of February 7 that the wind turned southward and sent the fire toward the waterfront and away from the city hall, courthouse, and other government buildings. In all, the fire caused an estimated $150 million in damage. By 5 p.m. on Monday, February 8, thirty hours after the initial alarm, the fire that was fought with fifty-seven engines, nine trucks, two hose companies, one fireboat, and one police boat was under control. It would be weeks before all the little pockets of smoldering ashes were extinguished.

The Shot Tower, Carroll Mansion, Little Italy, and the Flag House survived the fire. The old Manufacturer's Building and Trust bank building on Redwood Street made it through and is now the Springhill Suites hotel—and, yes, the old vault is still in the basement and is used for secure board and executive meetings.

It's difficult to understand how so much equipment and manpower from so many fire companies from as many as two hundred miles away couldn't control or extinguish the conflagration more quickly—that is, until you realize that the most notable impediment to knocking down the fire more quickly was that the equipment didn't match.

In Mary Ellen Hayward's book *The Architecture of Baltimore*, she notes that there were "over 600 sizes and variations of fire hose couplings in the United States" at the time. According to the Fire Research Division of the Building and Fire Research Laboratory,

> *When fire hoses were first manufactured, the threads that were used to couple them differed among all the manufacturers. The same was true for fire hydrant connections. Since the first fire hydrant was designed in 1817 by George Smith, each design, including hose connection threads, was patented by its manufacturer. Differences in hose connections on the hydrants, both diameters and threads, were part of the design that protected manufacturers from competition. Cities with different hydrant suppliers had fire fighting water supply systems with connections that were incompatible with those in other—sometimes neighboring—communities. History demonstrates that in major urban fires, the inability of fire fighting apparatus from other areas to utilize the water supply, because of incompatible hose connections, was a contributing factor to increased fire damage.*

There were no national standards and by the time standards were recommended for hose and hydrant hookups, too many cities had invested too much money in the purchase and infrastructure of hydrants and fire equipment to go back to the drawing board.

Robert Williams, assistant director of the Fire Museum of Maryland, says that another factor adding fuel to the fire, so to speak, was the tangle of overhead wires that crisscrossed every street. They diffused the water spray from the hoses and they (and many store-front awnings) prevented equipment from being moved into place. The wires were excellent conduits for the flames to jump from one building to the next. And then they were coated in ice as the water froze in the frigid air. Some wires snapped, before electric power was cut to them, and created still another hazard for safety personnel and machines. Additionally, building codes with fireproof or fire-resistant standards had not been established or enacted. The windows broke easily from the heat and firebrands flew from one building into the open windows of the next, setting it on fire. Furthermore, buildings were built one on top of the other.

One miraculous "truth" has been told since the fire: no one died during it. In Peter B. Peterson's book *The Great Baltimore Fire,* he notes that James Collins, a Johns Hopkins University undergradu-ate, researched the fire for his senior thesis in 2003 and found "a tiny, three-inch story titled 'One Life Lost in Fire'" in the *Baltimore Sun.* It said, "The charred remains of an African-American man was retrieved from the basin [now known as the inner harbor] at Bow-ley's Wharf" by Navy guardsmen on patrol duty. Four or five people are said to have died indirectly, including two men from the Fourth Regiment of the Maryland National Guard who died of pneumonia, and two firefighters who died of pneumonia and tuberculosis.

As a result of the fire, city building codes were improved and enforced, calling for more fire-resistant and fireproof materials. Streets that at thirty to forty feet wide were too narrow for fire equipment were widened. Electrical lines were buried underground, a pressurized water supply system was created, and the sewer system was modernized. Amazingly, the city was rebuilt and restored enough within two years that a huge festival was held to honor and celebrate the accomplishments and improvements.

In 1991, nine decades after the Great Baltimore Fire, hose incompatibility contributed to the extensive damage in the Oakland Hills firestorm in California. Whereas the standard hose coupling now has a diameter of 2.5 inches, Oakland's hydrants had 3-inch couplings. Following the fire, which claimed 25 lives, nearly 2,500 single-family homes, and 437 apartments, and caused more than $1.5 billion in damages, the fire hydrants were replaced, using the recommended specifications for hose connections.

Even now the Building and Fire Research Laboratory reports, "More than one hundred years after the fire and the adoption of a national standard for fire hydrant connections, (only) 18 out of the 48 most populated U.S. cities have both small hose and pumper connections on fire hydrants that comply with the NFPA standard." Baltimore is one of the eighteen.

Ironically, "in the process of establishing fundamental standards and planning basic research programs, the National Bureau of Standards (NBS), now the National Institute of Standards and Technology (NIST), encountered in late 1904 the same incompatibility of hose couplings that firefighters had during the Baltimore fire. One evening, while trying to put out a small fire, Franklin Durston, a NBS employee, found out that the hoses in the North and South Buildings of NBS could not be coupled because of different threads."

Although the Great Chicago Fire in 1871 and the 1906 San Francisco earthquake and fire are both better known and each had more fire-related fatalities, it was the Baltimore fire that was credited with the push toward stricter building codes and the adoption of fire equipment standards. Also, it's thought that misplaced smoldering smoking material caused the fire in Charm City, and that is not as romantic or interesting as the tale of Mrs. O'Leary's cow or an earthquake.

BOOKMOBILES

1905

Even with today's one-two-three punch of easy and almost universal Internet access, the decline of the independent bookstore, and ever-tightening budgets, the report of the death of public libraries seems to have been, as Mark Twain would say, "greatly exaggerated."

Similarly, the decline of personal and attentive service is put into sharp relief when you encounter library staff members that will answer your questions even when the libraries are closed, and in ways to make sure you have books even if you can't get to your library in person. This kind of consideration is sorely lacking in many businesses today.

Public library access was not always easy. They were located in highly populated areas, which could be difficult to reach for those who had limited access to public transportation. The library was for the elite, who could read and afford private transportation.

Mary Lemist Titcomb (1857–1931) was Washington County's first librarian, credited with creating the first book wagon in 1905 so homes and children throughout even the most rural part of the county could have access to books. The wagon was filled with books and traveled from Hagerstown to the remote areas within the county. She had been working toward this goal when she established branch libraries a year earlier, located in general stores and local post offices. Boxes of assorted books were sent to each deposit station (a mini branch or field library), but she wanted more.

Titcomb convinced the library trustees that a well-stocked wagon visiting the neighborhoods and carrying large numbers of books would be a goodwill gesture. Once the price of the wagon was covered, she told them, the upkeep would be the same as the system of dropping off books at the deposit stations.

She was concerned that the wagon might resemble a laundry wagon or a hearse, or "dead wagon," so she didn't want a fancy paint job. A wagon was assembled, painted, stocked with books on the exterior shelving, and teamed with a pair of horses led by Joshua Thomas. By April 1905, the innovative service was on its way.

Regrettably, that first wagon, its contents, and for a little while Titcomb's project, were shattered when a train ran into it in 1910. The concept had proven so successful, though, that a motorized wagon replaced it in 1912, then itself was replaced in the 1920s, 1930s, 1950s, and 1960s. From 1969 to 1985 another bus served and most recently, a new bus that's the size of a public bus or large motor home still delivers books to rural areas, senior living facilities, day care centers, Head Start programs, and other stops throughout Washington County.

Today's Washington County bookmobile, which is wheelchair accessible, carries about four thousand books, large-print books, magazines, and audiobooks. Most of the material is geared toward the younger set and senior citizens and is supplemented by items patrons request. Books are also delivered to those who are home-bound and in those cases where the bookmobile can't drive to a location; a box of books is taken to a deposit site for distribution. The mobile library stops at each location once a month, and no fees are charged for late returns.

Although it took a while, the success of the Washington County book wagon spread to other jurisdictions. The first horse-drawn moving library in Baltimore, part of the Enoch Pratt Free Library, started making the rounds in 1941 with nine thousand books on board. The system worked to make sure books were available to the population, particularly as the country fought in World War II and individuals had limited access to private cars and fuel. Within the first year, more than 132,000 books circulated.

The Wicomico Public Library system bought its first book-mobile in 1948 for $3,000, according to a report in *The Crab,* the Maryland state librarians' publication. The system brought its sixth bookmobile on board in February 2007 and uses it "six days a week, stopping at twelve schools; thirty-two daycare centers; eight senior and other service centers; five Head Start, Family Support and Latch-key Centers; and 18 other places. The annual circulation is 56,100 books, magazines and videos." That was a 10 percent increase over the previous year. This one had a price tag of $175,000, a bargain, according to library director Tom Hehman, before a price increase that would have added another $70,000. The fifth vehicle had logged 120,000 miles during its fifteen years of service.

Washington County still provides bookmobile service and dispatches a smaller van to places that don't need the larger bookmobile or whose location doesn't allow the bookmobile to maneuver properly. Allegany, Baltimore, Calvert, Caroline, Carroll, Cecil, Charles, Harford, and Talbot counties all have bookmobiles or other outreach programs. Other jurisdictions, including Caroline, Queen Anne's, Dorchester, Montgomery, and Worcester counties, and Baltimore City, provide books by mail to people who cannot visit the library.

Dorchester County did have a bookmobile but due to budgetary constraints ceased operating it on July 17, 2011.

Titcomb's exploits and successes were covered in a paper she wrote, "The Story of the Washington County Free Library," for a 1909 presentation to the American Library Association. The traveling-library idea was copied by jurisdictions across the country and around the world. Some delivery systems are a little different even today, with books being delivered by boats and ships (Norway), buses, camels (Uganda), donkeys, elephants (Thailand), wheelbarrows, and vans.

Nationally, bookmobile popularity peaked and waned at not quite an inverse ratio to the growth in Internet access, but as a part ebb and flow of the popularity of the library world in general. From 1990 to 2005 the number of bookmobiles dropped from more than 1,100 to 825 and then, according to a 2010 report by the American Library Association, the number in the United States started to increase again, reaching 930 in 2008. One reason given for the increase is that even though a bookmobile may cost around $200,000, it's a lot cheaper than building a new library, which averages around $1.6 million. Kentucky is said to have the most bookmobiles with 98, followed by California with 69. Hawaii, Alaska, and Oklahoma each have only one. There are enough delivery and other services that librarians have formed an Association of Bookmobile and Outreach Services organization, and National Bookmobile Day is celebrated on the Wednesday of National Library Week every April.

Titcomb's innovative approach to reaching people who couldn't otherwise access a library was stretched to another national (and perhaps international) first in 2007 when two bookmobiles were delivered to the state's correctional education libraries services. These serve inmates in the prerelease prisons, where they live before being returned to the community. The bookmobiles visit the Western Correctional institution and sixteen other state prison libraries and carry information about housing, jobs, credit restoration, community services, reconnecting with their families, and just navigating a system that has radically changed. "Many of these inmates have never used a computer or accessed the Internet." Each vehicle has five computers and other equipment. Glennor Shirley, state library coordinator for state prison libraries, said in *The Crab,* "I am not aware of any other prison library bookmobile in the country."

PROHIBITION

1919

The Wartime Prohibition Act, calling for an end to producing alcoholic beverages as a way to conserve grain for our troops battling in World War I, took effect nationally on January 17, 1920. Yes, that was more than a year after the war ended, but Congress didn't even enact it until November 18, 1918, which also was after the war was over. In Maryland, according to the state's historical society, Prohibition started on June 30, 1919, when the act took effect.

Prohibition in Maryland ran a wobbly course, at best, but it has continued to have major effects on our state and our lives. Despite heavy objections from Baltimore City, where 72 percent of the voters rejected the idea in a 1916 referendum, Maryland was the sixth state to ratify the Eighteenth Amendment in February 1918. That probably was the last resounding support for the measure, because for numerous reasons, nearly half of the state senators, almost 90 percent of the delegates, and sitting governor Emerson C. Harrington were defeated by the time enforcement began. Albert C. Ritchie, who opposed Prohibition, was the victorious gubernatorial candidate, stating that the issue was one of states' rights. Together the governor and legislature refrained from passing a state prohibition law, making Maryland the only state that did not enact such legislation.

One current daily reminder of the "dry" days came through the *Baltimore Sun,* which said Prohibition endangered the Tenth Amendment, which protected states' rights. Through frequent use of the phrase "Maryland Free State" in editorials in the *Sun,* editor Hamilton Owens helped coin the Maryland nickname of the "Free State," which is still in use today. The nickname had nothing to do with slavery, which had been abolished more than five decades earlier.

As thinking people might have guessed, because the Volstead Act (named for Andrew Volstead, Republican from Minnesota and chair of the House Judiciary Committee) allowed people to keep whatever they already had in their homes, people bought all the alcoholic beverages they could, storing it in closets or basements before the measure took effect. Wholesalers bought huge supplies, loading ships at Sparrows Point, and sending it to warehouses in Nassau.

Prohibition was not welcomed quietly in Maryland, as the *Baltimore Sun* continued to condemn the law and Congressmen Vincent Palmisano, John Philip Hill, and Millard E. Tydings repeatedly submitted legislation to repeal the act. Hill, educated at Johns Hopkins and Harvard Universities, lived in a large home with an equally large backyard where he planted apple trees and grapevines, from which he reaped a cellarful of their liquid products. He was tried in 1924 for violating the Volstead Act but Judge Morris A. Soper threw out the charges.

On December 5, 2007, seventy-four years after the repeal, Brandon Arnold, director of government affairs at the Cato Institute in Washington, D.C., commented about the legacy of Prohibition in Maryland and the thirteen years the nation was dry. Arnold says, "As the only constitutional amendment ever repealed, history confirms that the Eighteenth Amendment was an abject failure. . . . Prohibition reduced alcohol consumption only moderately, but led to a dramatic increase in crime and corruption. Organized crime flourished, and bootlegging, rum running and smuggling became commonplace—especially in Baltimore, where resistance to Prohibition was strong."

Baltimore was a hot spot of speakeasies, which were raided by federal agents on a regular basis only to reopen almost like the Lernaean Hydra, the beast (and guardian to the entrance of the underworld) of Greek mythology that grew two heads for each one that was cut off.

Although the counties from the Eastern Shore and western Maryland had been almost unanimously in favor of Prohibition, cities and farms in other parts of the state were home to distilleries and breweries where stills were large enough to produce thousands of gallons of the illegal liquid. A large operation, the Blue Blazes Whiskey Still, was set in what is now Catoctin Mountain Park in Frederick County and "used a boiler from a steam locomotive, had thirteen 2,000-gallon fermenting vats, and produced enough moonshine to supply all of the speakeasies in Philadelphia, Baltimore, and Washington, D.C.," reported Bob Janiskee in an article about the park. (The still was destroyed in 1929, but demonstrations using other equipment were given regularly until 1989, when the still's permit was revoked. A self-guided informational tour is available today.)

In a *Baltimore Sun* article, Jacques Kelly says, "People who never drank started making their own wine. Certainly our Guilford Avenue neighbors did." In the mid-1960s, he says, "I was helping some neighbors, on the same block, clean out an old cellar. There, under the front porch, was a dust-covered still, copper tubing and all."

Most people today probably have heard of the Women's Christian Temperance Union as a primary supporter of Prohibition.

Marylanders, living in what was known as one of the "wettest" states in the country, heard from the vocal members of the Association Against the Prohibition Amendment and the Women's Organization for National Prohibition Reform. Except for the voters of Dorchester County, the rest of the state's electorate voted on September 12, 1933, to repeal and within a few months beer was available for public sale within the state.

A major leftover from the repeal was the establishment of three-tiered distribution systems that were in effect in Maryland until legislation was enacted in 2011 that allows wineries to ship wine directly to Maryland residents.

Even with the bill, Arnold says the "three-tiered distribution system still limits what can be delivered to Maryland residents. They cannot receive beer directly from brewers and it's still limited in scope. They can't buy wine or beer from a grocery store." Under this type of system, says Arnold, "producers cannot sell their wares directly to consumers. In fact, they cannot even sell directly to grocery stores, restaurants or other retailers. Instead, they are required . . . to sell their products to wholesalers, who in turn sell to retailers, who then sell to consumers. Of course, each step in the process leads to an additional markup so in the end, consumers spend a lot more for the beer, wine or spirits than they should."

Arnold says many Marylanders work in Washington and just have alcoholic products shipped to their offices. Although wholesalers have a lot of influence in the Maryland legislature, this obviously significantly reduces tax revenue the state would receive if the shipments came in through Maryland. The new measure says only wineries, not retailers, can ship to Maryland residences. Supporters of wider licenses, including the group called Marylanders for Better Beer and Wine Laws, want the right to include retailers (e.g., *New York Times, Wall Street Journal,* and other brick-and-mortar businesses) who have wine-of-the-month clubs. Some would also like to include distributors so they could ship foreign wines that are not available in the United States.

Although because of its stand against Prohibition Maryland took on the nickname of the "Free State," it's ironic that residents are not free to buy the alcoholic beverages they want where it is most convenient.

DESIRE OF THE ELMS

1931

If, as they say, "you are of an age"—meaning you're old enough and you grew up in a Capraesque town or visited such old European cities as Paris and Edinburgh before the mid-'70s—you remember the majestic elm trees. They lined the grand boulevards and main streets of towns and cities big and small and filled parks and gardens. You remember walking along Elm Street, sitting under a shady, leafy green umbrella on a lazy day. These deciduous trees, particularly the American elm *(Ulmus americana),* grow quickly and are stately, and tall (up to one hundred feet or even more). They live long lives (up to four hundred years) and are nicely shaped, creating a lovely canopy. They also can withstand the stress of an urban environment.

By the late 1960s the evidence was obvious that the trees were dying from the fungus *Ophiostoma ulmi,* or Dutch elm disease (DED). As many as 95 percent of the trees died, generally very quickly. For people with those memories and those too young to have them, rejoice for the elm tree is returning.

Calling the fungus that is spread by three varieties of elm bark beetles a Dutch disease did a great disservice to that country, for it was merely Dutch scientists who first identified the problem in 1921. DED spread from there throughout Europe and originally was thought to have come out of the Himalayas, but then was determined to have begun in France.

The disease came to the United States in 1931 through infected elm logs from France used as veneer by a Cleveland, Ohio, furniture company. In 1945, during World War II, the disease invaded Canada with a second establishment of the infection. Over the next five decades, it slowly but inexorably spread throughout most areas with deciduous trees in forests and in populated areas. It was found in Detroit by 1950, Chicago by 1960, and Minneapolis by 1970. By the 1980s about seventy-seven million trees had been attacked. It was a *Nightmare on Elm Street* without Johnny Depp.

Research on finding ways to control or eliminate the disease and the beetle, developing tree barks that are unattractive to the beetles, and determining whether any elm varieties are immune to the fungus started shortly after the infestations and has been conducted with some success in Japan, Italy, Canada, and other countries.

Denny Townsend, a geneticist, led the effort to find DED-resistant trees in a project by scientists at the US Agricultural Research Service, the National Arboretum in Washington, D.C. (operated by the ARS), and the Floral and Nursery Plants Research Unit at Glenn Dale, Maryland. Together with horticulturalist Susan Bentz and National Park Service plant pathologist James L. Sherald they screened thousands of American elm trees and found enough specimens to start breeding and producing DED-tolerant trees. A tree from the National Mall in Washington, D.C.—one of about three hundred that had been planted along the Mall in the 1930s—that had survived an attack of the fungus was cloned in 1993, and in

2005, the year Townsend retired, ARS released an American elm variety called Jefferson. At maturity it stands as much as sixty-eight feet tall with dark green leaves that last late into the fall. You can see the results of the team's work in Jefferson elm trees planted on the National Mall and at the arboretum, and a Valley Forge American elm on the grounds of the US Capitol. Soon you will see them return to more public and private settings as well.

Through their research, botanist Alan T. Whittemore and geneticist Richard T. Olsen, the ARS scientists, and other collaborators discovered American elm trees that seem to hold the secret to resisting the disease. Getting a little technical, the trees are diploid (elm trees with two copies of chromosomes), triploids (three copies of the chromosomes), and tetraploid (four copies of the chromosomes). The tetraploid trees are most susceptible to the disease. However, it wasn't until this round of research that the scientists even found the diploid trees, thinking originally that the triploids—for example, the Jefferson—were just an aberration. Suddenly the thought was that if tetraploids and triploids exist, there must be diploids that over the years have diverged enough to be significantly different.

Within the United States, four cultivars of the elm tree are showing promise as highly resistant: the Princeton, Jefferson, Valley Forge, and the New Harmony. Eight other elm trees (Prospector, Frontier, Homestead, Pioneer, Patriot, Ohio, Pathfinder, and Dynasty) that were bred from Asian and European species have been introduced and released to plant nurseries. None is totally disease resistant, particularly if the tree is stressed by drought or weakened by other diseases.

Part of the problem is that when gardeners use the same tools to remove diseased trees and then to prune healthy trees, the fungus spreads. Disinfecting the tools with even a weak solution of sodium hypochlorite, lye, oxygen bleach, and calcium hypochlorite (household chlorine bleach) before using them on disease-free trees is essential. Some jurisdictions prohibit pruning from early spring through late fall because the cuts would be easily invaded by the bark beetles.

However, the new trees provide genetic diversity to the trees that reproduce through wind-blown seeds that float in the breeze and then settle on the ground. Occasionally the trees also are pollinated by visiting bees.

Elm trees have shown their popularity even with their old, nasty reputation. They still play a popular and important part of the plant nursery business, to the tune of nearly $5 billion a year. They've come along at an opportune moment, as trees that were planted to replace the elms are succumbing to their own problems. Although it takes about a dozen years to bring elm trees to market age, nurseries are starting to add them to their stock and some Home Depot stores along the Eastern Shore carry them for about $100 to nearly $300, depending on the size and age of the tree.

It has taken almost a century to overcome the damage from the infected wood imported from France to Ohio, but their revival is occurring just as many people are jumping on the "Made in America" bandwagon. Fortunately, part of that movement can be promoting these American trees and the return of our horticultural history—putting elm trees back on Elm Streets.

AN ILL WIND BLOWS GOOD

1933

More than 300,000 people fill the nearly ten miles of Ocean City's Atlantic coastline every summer weekend for a total of eight million a year. These crowds seem as normal as a sunburn after a day at the beach. Everyone there hopes for clear skies and cool breezes.

Yet, it was a big rain and an ill wind that helped create the Ocean City we know.

Tides and winds had helped form the seaside town, part of a long north–south barrier island that ran from Delaware to several miles south of Ocean City. The Algonquians visited and lived here, enjoying the abundant food supply long before European settlers came to town. Giovanni de Verrazano sailed along and explored the East Coast in 1524 and the bridge on Route 611 from the mainland to Assateague State Park is named in his honor (as is the Verrazano Narrows Bridge in New York City). Sometime during the seventeenth century, European settlers moved north from Virginia.

Developers started building guest cottages as early as 1869, and the four hundred–room Victorian-style Atlantic Hotel opened on

July 4, 1875. With more people came the need for more services and a railroad bridge was built across Sinepuxent Bay in 1876 and the US Life-Saving Service (today's Coast Guard) was established here in 1878. Ferry service became available that connected Maryland's Western Shore across the Chesapeake Bay to the Eastern Shore, making the beaches readily available for visitors from Baltimore, Annapolis, and Washington, D.C.

Then an ill wind started on August 17, 1933, in the central Atlantic Ocean, northeast of the Leeward Islands, typical of August storms that feed on the warm ocean waters. It skirted south of Bermuda and continued on a west by northwest track until it made landfall on early August 22 north of Cape Hatteras, North Carolina, a little south of Virginia Beach, Virginia. It reached a top wind speed of 120 miles per hour, making it a category 3 storm on today's Saffir-Simpson Hurricane Scale.

Tropical storms received official names with the onset of Bess in 1949, so the designation for the hurricane that reached Ocean City on August 23, 1933, was Hurricane 8, later to be referred to as the Chesapeake-Potomac Hurricane. And although it carried the name Hurricane 8, technically it was the eighth tropical storm and the third hurricane of the 1933 hurricane season. It was the first year, since records were kept, to have this many storms this early, until 2005 when Tropical Storm Harvey developed on August 2.

As Hurricane 8 spun its way up the coast, the storm surge it produced became higher and higher, first pushing Chesapeake Bay waters inland and then the waters of the Potomac River. Additionally, the storm dumped up to ten inches of rain a day along the Potomac River, Chesapeake Bay, and Delmarva Peninsula. Some reports indicate the storm swept a train off the Anacostia River trestle; later research indicated the support under the pilings had been eroding away and the rain, winds, and tide caused the trestle to collapse. Regardless, ten people died when the train fell into the river. The path Hurricane 8 took was nearly duplicated by Hurricane Isabel seventy years later in 2003, a storm that also left massive destruction in the mid-Atlantic states.

Although the storm claimed only thirty lives (none in Ocean City), it was responsible for sinking or damaging hundreds of boats. Chesapeake Beach, in Calvert County on the western shore of the bay, had been a thriving vacation town with a ballroom, picnicking, amusements, camping, and a half-mile-long pier that received steamboats filled with pleasure seekers from Baltimore. The resort was an hour's train ride from Washington, D.C. Its developers saw it as a nearby alternative to more distant resorts, such as New Jersey's Atlantic City and New York's Coney Island—that is until Hurricane 8. It consumed the ballroom, amusement park, concession stands, and pier. Just a stone's throw away in North Beach, where the Chesapeake Beach employees lived, the storm wiped out nearly six dozen summer homes.

A mile-long piece of Ocean City's seasonal boardwalk that had been started sometime between 1900 and 1902 was lost to history, as was the railroad bridge. Much of the infrastructure and popular amusements of Public Landing, a small village south of Ocean City, were destroyed in the storm and although the pier and waterfront activity were reestablished, it never regained its popularity.

By August 26, 1933, the worst storm to hit the area in more than a century was spent, but not before causing more than $27 million (in 1933 USD; $461 million in 2010 USD) in damage. Much of the damage was to buildings and boats, but crops also suffered, all blows that added hardship to those who were already distressed from the Great Depression.

In its wake, the storm created massive runoff and overflow from creeks, lakes, and rivers. Winds had died down but still were clocked at up to eighty miles per hour. Tides reached seven feet and more over flood stage. All the elements merged to besiege Ocean City, cutting a fifty-foot path from Sinepuxent Bay through the sandbar to the Atlantic. This was the start of the massive change that has overtaken those barrier islands; this passageway allows work and pleasure boats to enter sheltered waters while providing easy access to deep water.

Following the 1933 storm, Assateague was a separate thirty-seven-mile barrier island spanning the Maryland/Virginia border. Much as tides come and go, interest in establishing a national seashore ran hot and cold, with discussions going on for years. Eventually a section in Maryland was platted for development with a road, Baltimore Boulevard, paved. Before any buildings could be constructed, another storm came through in 1962 and ruined most of the road and many of the buildings that were already on the island. Some people felt the gods were on Nature's side. Finally federal legislation was enacted in 1965 approving the Assateague Island National Seashore.

Local residents and business owners, particularly those involved in the fishing and boat industry, for years had been requesting a cut-through. The souvenir left by Hurricane 8 was the impetus they needed to make it a reality. It took two years for US Senator Millard E. Tydings (D-MD) to persuade the government to finance a permanent cut-through, now called the inlet, that separated Ocean City from Assateague Island with a system of artificial jetties. Without them the sand would once again silt and sift back to the island and block the inlet. With this access, the Sinepuxent Bay side of Ocean City has seen increased development, and over the years Ocean City has grown in year-round population and summer popularity, all from an ill wind that swept the area in 1933.

WEDDING CAPITAL OF THE EAST

1938

The reasons for a town's fame and growth can be a seam of coal, a deepwater harbor, or an inconsiderate aquarium owner tossing a pair of northern Chinese snakehead fish into a local pond. Sometimes the fame is fleeting and other times it takes on a life of its own.

In the case of Elkton, the Cecil County seat, fame came as the Wedding Capital of the East in 1913 when the Delaware legislature enacted a marriage waiting period similar to laws in other states along the Atlantic coast.

Couples from New York, New Jersey, Pennsylvania, and the New England states who wanted to marry quickly suddenly had to travel to Maryland to avoid a waiting period, a residency requirement, or prerequisite for blood tests. Elkton was the closest county seat south of those northern states where couples could be married without waiting.

Mike Dixon, Cecil County historian, says officials in the First State even told people to go "sixteen to eighteen miles down the road to Elkton to be married."

All you had to do was be married by a member of the clergy (Maryland was the last state to authorize civil marriages, effective January 1, 1964).

A cottage industry of wedding chapels sprung up almost overnight with fifteen of them lining Main Street and side lanes at its heyday. Elkton became the Gretna Green (the Scotland village where impetuous couples would go because as long as the boy was fourteen and the girl was twelve, they did not need parental permission to wed) of America.

As many as twelve thousand couples tied the knot every year, in a town of about three thousand. Dixon says statistically, if just locals were married, it would have amounted to about 150 a year. This is where Babe Ruth, Willie Mays, Cornel Wilde, Billie Holiday, Debbie Reynolds, Martha Raye, the Rev. Pat Robertson, Irving Lahrheim (Bert Lahr), Joan Fontaine, Charles Barkley, and former US Attorney General John Mitchell and his second wife, Martha Beall Mitchell, were married.

There were conditions, one hundred pages of them, says Dixon. And anyone could easily squeak around them. If one or both parties was underage, a simple statement that the guy was headed into the military or the gal was pregnant—local doctors would provide a certificate attesting to that—and the age minimum was waived. A few doctors ultimately were indicted for their shenanigans.

Trains, referred to as the Honeymoon Express, pulled into the station regularly. Taxicab drivers staked out a position at the train station and greeted the couples, touting a package deal that included a stop at the courthouse, a visit to a floral shop, and on to the chapel. Yes, the cab drivers and parsons were in cahoots.

The fact that the train station was only two blocks from the center of town and the cabbies charged $20 riled the city and county fathers, says Jessica Price, administrative assistant of the

Elkton Chamber of Commerce and Alliance. Enough was enough, according to Dixon. Nearly twenty pages of taxicab restrictions were enacted, dictating what they could and could not do. The local police started cracking down on the cabbies, trying to stop their entrepreneurial ways.

At one point, Dixon says, in the late '30s the police became so zealous that they stopped the speeding town car carrying the Iranian ambassador. Apparently "the new police chief, Jack Biddle, blew his whistle for the driver to stop. He didn't notice the flags waving on the front of the car or the diplomatic license plate. The driver said the man was a minister, the chief thought meant he was a man of the cloth rather than a political figure."

The town's image and reputation were starting to tarnish, becoming thought of as tawdry and perhaps even tasteless. Except by the 1930s, with the country still reeling from the Depression, all these weddings were bringing in a bundle of money from the chapels, restaurants, florists, motels, and other shops and businesses in the area.

Business or no, an almost lethal blow fell upon Elkton on December 7, 1938, as state voters adopted a referendum approving a forty-eight-hour waiting period (Cecil County overwhelmingly voted it down, to no avail). The number of wedding couples also declined as Las Vegas became a more attractive wedding destination because of the resorts, casinos, and other venues. Another near-fatal blow came when the state routed through traffic off of Main Street and onto the newly constructed Maryland Route 40 that bypassed the town. In all, the December 1938 figures for couples coming to Elkton to be married had dropped by 90 percent from October and November.

Today the town's population is closer to fourteen thousand or fifteen thousand. The Little Wedding Chapel, a quaint Federal-style stone structure built in 1813, with six pews seating about thirty people, is the only reminder of the chapels that once were. Janice Potts, deputy clerk of the court, says the county issues 1,200 or more marriage certificates a year, counting civil ceremonies she performs and those done by the clergy. Some of the couples are local residents and some are the children or grandchildren of people who were married here.

Part of the early and continued popularity came from Hollywood movie makers and TV script writers. If you have seen such movies as *The Manchurian Candidate* (1962, with Frank Sinatra, Laurence Harvey, and Janet Leigh), *Guys and Dolls, The Philadelphia Story, Pillow Talk,* and *Solid Gold Cadillac,* then you've heard people talking about eloping to Elkton or going to "that town in Maryland" to get married. Trivia fiend and friend Bob Cullen remembers scenes from *I Dream of Jeannie* and *Welcome Back Kotter* that mentioned traveling to Maryland to get married. Dixon remembers a mention on *The Waltons.* What's strange about the first two is that they took place and were aired long after the quickie weddings had stopped, and *Jeannie* took place in Florida, and it would probably be a stretch to come this far north for a wedding. Yes, the memory does persist.

The train doesn't stop in Elkton anymore. The mayor and city fathers (and mothers) are trying to convince MARC (Maryland Area Regional Commuter) officials to extend the line from Perryville to Elkton and SEPTA (Southeastern Pennsylvania Transportation Authority) officials to extend their line traveling from and to Philadelphia to assist commuters traveling to Baltimore and points south and Philadelphia to the north.

Today the county and town delight in the wedding capital reputation. A marker designating the town as the Wedding Capital of the East was installed and unveiled in front of the Chapel (it's a specific chapel, not generic) on June 2, 2007, and early in 2011 the

Historical Society of Cecil County created a program exploring this piece of history. Since sometime in the 1990s, the Chamber holds an annual wedding and renewal event on the second Friday of June (National Marriage Day) where five to fifteen couples exchange vows for the first or umpteenth time. One couple was married there in 2005 and has returned annually to participate in the vow-renewal program. Wedding cake and hors d'oeuvres are served and a horse-drawn carriage helps complete the romantic image.

FLYING BOXCAR

1944

Prior to World War II, flying cargo from one place to another within the country and across the ocean was limited to items that could fit inside the plane through a rather small side cargo door or items that could be broken down to go through the door.

In response to military demands as the war progressed, the Fairchild Aircraft Company in Hagerstown developed a new plane dubbed the Flying Boxcar. It was unique, says Tom Riford, president and CEO of the Hagerstown-Washington County Convention and Visitors Bureau, because its interior dimension was the size of a train boxcar. Even more unusual, it had a hinged rear door and an uninterrupted interior cargo hold that allowed bulky equipment and personnel to load from ground level through the tail. Previously cargo was stowed from an elevated level at the side of the plane. The plane was purpose-built rather than converting civilian planes to military purposes. Its predecessor, the XC-31, was a side-loading aircraft that also was unique in design because the floor of the plane was four feet above ground level, the same height as flatbed trucks.

Under the existing construction system, Fairchild would have had to build a large number of extensive factories. Instead, says Riford, they "started using a process that would be called the Hagerstown System. Instead of Fairchild building factories at the Hagerstown airport that would consume time, funds, and space, they started using and repurposing local factories and companies."

Among the twenty-seven local firms that were converted to supply Fairchild were the Brandt Cabinet Works (wooden fabrication and welding of aluminum sections for the planes), Beachley Furniture Company (wooden parts and sections), Statton Furniture Manufacturing Company, Hagerstown Leather Company, Maryland Motors, Hess Auto Body Works, and the Foltz Manufacturing and Supply Company.

The Moller Pipe Organ Works (the world's largest manufacturer of pipe organs) made 3,400 wing panels and 2,000 center sections for the PT-19. Even the large Exhibition Hall of the Hagerstown Fairgrounds, which used to hold poultry shows, was converted to production and fabrication. About 1,200 PT-19s were built between 1941 and 1944. In all, it's estimated that Fairchild employed between 80 percent and 90 percent of the town's workforce in one capacity or another, involving more than fifty thousand people.

The twin-tailed plane had two Pratt & Whitney R2800 engines that delivered 2,100 horsepower, and Fairchild coordinated with the Air Force and Troop Carrier Command in its design. Within a short time it was determined that the plane was underpowered and wasn't strong enough to carry the loads it needed to bear. An amped-up version, the XC-82B, incorporated engines with 2,650 horsepower, 550 more than the C-82, and had a wider and stronger fuselage. It became the C-119, which was also modified several times for specific uses. The new plane could carry twelve tons of men and equipment (up from about ten tons) and fly up to 1,500 miles nonstop. It could be converted to carry thirty-six litter patients and attendant personnel. Other changes included moving the cockpit from over the cargo area (which restricted pilot visibility) to a more forward position, flush with the nose. This allowed the C-119 to carry still more cargo and decreased the amount of runway required for takeoff. About 1,100 of them were built.

Among its other uses, a 1953 C-119G was used by the Canadian Air Force and as a fire bomber. According to netNebraska, the state's PBS station, the C-82 was also used over the winter of 1948–1949 after an intense blizzard that blanketed Nebraska and three other states so thoroughly that ranchers couldn't reach their cattle to feed them. Other wildlife, including deer, also were starving. The C-82s, with some C-47s, dropped an estimated fifty thousand tons of hay bales from low-altitude flights, and it's estimated that more than four million cattle were saved from starvation and nearly a quarter million people were rescued. Although not heavily involved, the C-82s also were used in the Berlin airlift in 1948 and 1949, when the Soviet Union blocked train and vehicle access to Berlin in an attempt to gain control over the entire city. Along with other cargo planes, more than 200,000 flights were made, providing nearly five thousand tons of fuel, food, and other daily necessities.

The National Air and Space Administration used a modified C-119 to retrieve space capsules as they returned to earth. It also became a staple as an air tanker or water bomber fighting wildfires. The US Air Force Strategic Air Command employed the C-119 to recover high-altitude balloon-carried instrument packages at the onset of the Corona spy satellite program. The French used the planes—secretly loaned to them by the CIA—in their battles in Vietnam, playing a critical part in providing supplies to French troops at Dien Bien Phu.

Besides use by the various components of the US Air Force, the C-119 was used by the air wings of the military services of Belgium, Brazil, Ethiopia, India, Italy, Taiwan, and other countries. Domestically, they were used extensively in Alaska to provide supplies to people and villages that are inaccessible during the winter.

Although our memories of the Flying Boxcar may be dimming, movies help keep it alive. A C-119G from Canada was portrayed in the movie *Always* starring Holly Hunter and John Goodman, with Richard Dreyfuss as a firefighting pilot. A C-82 was used in the 1965 Jimmy Stewart film *Flight of the Phoenix* (which used three C-82 planes for filming). Its newer relative, the C-119, was used in the 2004 remake of *Flight of the Phoenix,* starring Dennis Quaid. All of the planes were made in Hagerstown.

Rather than let the memory of the Hagerstown system plane disappear, the management of the Hagerstown Aviation Museum decided one should be added to what Riford says is the "largest collection of museum-owned rare and historic aircraft in Maryland." Museum staff heard about a plane that was going to be sold at auction by B&G Industries in Greybull, Wyoming. They quickly raised $140,000 and won the bid. Before it could travel, though, the plane needed to be evaluated and repaired for flying worthiness and brought up to FAA standards for the "ferry" flight. Some sixty years after the plane was built, only thirteen people still held qualifications to fly it, but only pilot Frank Lamm was still flying and willing to accept the responsibility of making sure the plane made the two thousand–mile trip successfully. His experience was with the Fairchild C-119, a second-generation Boxcar, so he had to receive FAA approval. He was joined by copilot T. R. Proven and flight engineer Jack Fastnaught, who also had extensive flying experience.

Other museums generally have aircraft that "are owned by individuals and loaned to the museum. The C-119G was donated because of the positive news that was generated when they gained possession of the C-82," says Kurtis Meyers, who was president of the Hagerstown Aviation Museum at the time. It includes a flyable one-fifth-scale replica of the PT-19 trainer. Until the Aviation Museum organization has a permanent home of its own, which Meyers says should happen by 2013, the aircraft are on display only at special events, such as the annual fall fly-in.

Sunday, October 15, 2006, was a "perfect sixty-eight degrees under a brilliant blue October sky when Lamm, Proven, and Fastnaught brought our historic icon back to the place of her birth," reports Meyers, "the first all-metal cargo aircraft specifically designed for the task. Fairchild built 223 of them between 1944 and 1948. This was the only one left in the entire world that was in relatively flyable 1945 condition." The trip home was arduous and circuitous. From Wyoming the flight took the three men to North Platte, Nebraska; Ottumwa, Iowa; and then to Culpeper, Virginia, before its last leg into Hagerstown. It was the plane's first flight in more than six years.

"Tons and tons of people" attended the plane's return, says Riford. They were former Fairchild employees and their descendants or friends of people who were involved in the company. Many had tears in their eyes as the plane flew over the factory where it was built and landed at the Hagerstown airport.

BLALOCK-TAUSSIG SHUNT

1944

Depending on the severity of the problem, if you were born with the congenital heart defect known as tetralogy of Fallot (TOF), or "blue baby" syndrome, prior to 1944, you might have died in infancy or perhaps lived until you were a teenager, although with blue lips, nose, toes, and fingers; shortness of breath; limited energy; and occasional fainting spells as a constant reminder of your condition. In all cases, there was no treatment, just inevitable death at an early age.

Fortunately, Johns Hopkins Hospital (the Johns has the "s" at the end of the name because Johns was the maiden name of the great-grandmother of the man who founded the hospital and medical school) was the place where so many medical practices were first implemented and adopted. Dr. William Osler, considered the "father of modern medicine," established the residency program, calling for new doctors to "reside" within the hospital. Hopkins was the first major medical school in the country to admit women as students equal to men, the first to use rubber gloves during surgery, and the first to develop renal dialysis for those suffering from kidney failure. Additionally, Constantin Fahlberg discovered the first synthetic sweetening agent, naming it

Saccharine, there on February 27, 1879. And Vitamin D was discovered, three types of polio virus were defined, and closed-heart massage (CPR) was developed at Johns Hopkins.

TOF, which happens in males slightly more frequently than in females, was first noted in 1672 by Niels Stensen, then in 1773 by Edward Sandifort and in 1888 by the French physician Étienne-Louis Arthur Fallot, for whom it is named.

It would be November 29, 1944, before a blue baby was saved through a surgical procedure referred to as the Blalock-Thomas-Taussig (or Blalock-Taussig) shunt. Surgeon Alfred Blalock, Vivien Thomas, Blalock's laboratory technician, and Dr. Helen B. Taussig, pediatric cardiologist (who later discovered thalidomide's damaging effects on fetuses and caused the drug to be banned from the United States), performed the first revolutionary surgery on a fifteen-month-old girl, Eileen Saxon. This procedure resolves the problem of a baby whose blood flow from the heart to the lungs is insufficient to oxygenate the blood, ergo, the appearance of blue skin.

Taussig graduated from the Johns Hopkins Medical School at a time when there weren't many women doctors. She was assigned to the cardiac care unit of the Harriet Lane Home for Invalid Children at Johns Hopkins. Children in the unit had heart disease from rheumatic fever (which attacked the heart valves) or congenital defects. Taussig was curious about those defects, and as unpleasant as it sounds, would ask the parents whether she could conduct an autopsy on the child to remove and preserve the heart. Soon doctors around the country would recommend that children with heart defects go to Hopkins. Taussig wasn't curing anyone yet, but she was helping them live longer and more productive lives.

Eventually, after treating hundreds of infants and children with this disorder, she wondered what would happen if the blood vessels near the heart were rearranged so they could provide more blood to the lungs so it could be better oxygenated. After conceiving a procedure that would eliminate the problem, she brought it to the attention of Blalock and Thomas in their Hopkins laboratory in 1943, suggesting that they should be able to shift the arteries around much "as a plumber changes pipes around." Blalock and Thomas had been experimenting with a procedure that rerouted the blood to the lungs. After extensive experimentation on dogs, they felt comfortable enough to try it—with success—on infants. At the time Thomas, an African American with only a high school diploma, was not given credit for his participation, though at the time it was not unusual for lab technicians to not be acknowledged.

Katie McCabe's 1989 article "Something the Lord Made" and the subsequent movie of the same name (starring Alan Rickman as Blalock, Mos Def as Thomas, and Mary Stuart Masterson as Taussig) and a 2003 PBS documentary, *Partners of the Heart*, highlighted Thomas's role in the surgical procedure's history.

The first patient, Eileen, weighed only nine pounds at the time of the surgery and the conditions were far from the nearly hermetically sealed surgical suites we see today. The operating room was on the top floor to allow natural light to flood through two large windows (it would soon be known as the Heart Room). Large cast-iron radiators provided heat. The ninety-minute surgery moved an artery that normally supplied blood to an arm, so that it went to the lungs.

This was long before people even thought about heart transplants or open-heart surgery. Occasionally a doctor would operate on a stab wound to the heart or to the pericardium that surrounds the heart. The heart itself, they thought, was too important to even consider invasive procedures.

This operation was done without benefit of historical precedence or instruction manuals. These doctors would write the books, and it was 1947 before Taussig wrote her first book, *Congenital*

Malformations of the Heart, and a second volume defining specific defects. Thomas also fabricated the miniaturize needles and clamps to make sure the sutures of the new connections would seal. The gratification was almost instantaneous, as the child's skin turned a normal pink as soon as the suturing was finished and the clamp that temporarily stopped the blood flow was released.

Eileen would need another surgical procedure but died shortly before her third birthday. Fourteen of the first seventy patients died, but the parents of the other children noted that fifty-six of them had lived. Eventually doctors stopped performing the procedure on infants unless they were in imminent danger of dying. However, the breakthrough operation started the practice of cardiac surgery. The concept of the procedure was so successful and word spread so rapidly that nearly a dozen other operations were performed within the next six months. By the time Blalock retired twenty years later, more than two thousand children had received the shunt at Hopkins and more than fifteen thousand had the lifesaving procedure worldwide.

The result was perhaps even more dramatic for older children who had lived fragile lives for so long. Following the procedure they could ride a bike, attend public school, dance at a prom, and do almost everything they would have been able to do if they hadn't had the defect. Regardless of the repair that improves their lifestyle and life span, they aren't cured or "fixed," because the original defect remains.

For those who had more serious congenital heart defects, this procedure allowed them to thrive long enough for more sophisticated open-heart surgeries to develop in the 1950s and 1960s.

Now, seven decades later, the procedure is still in use. Families of people with congenital heart disease celebrate November 29 as Red and Blue Day, asking supporters to dress in red and blue clothing to help promote additional research and cures for this disorder, which still takes more than three thousand American lives a year.

CHESAPEAKE BAY BRIDGE

1952

In the first half of the twentieth century, getting from the western side to the Eastern Shore of the Chesapeake Bay was a lengthy process. You either had to wait for a ferry or drive to the northernmost point of the bay, then go east and south to whatever the destination was on the other side. Ferries ran between Baltimore and Love Point, Annapolis and Matapeake, Annapolis and Claiborne (near St. Michaels), and Annapolis to Broad Creek on Kent Island. Eventually a ferry from Sandy Point as the western terminus instead of Annapolis to Matapeake shortened the water voyage.

A bridge idea is thought to have been proposed as early as the 1880s, and then again in 1907, that would mimic the ferry route that ran between Baltimore and Tolchester Beach, north of Rock Hall. The 155-acre area was a popular resort in Kent County that had an amusement park, hotel, dance hall, roller coaster, bingo, roller skating, a number of rides, and a wide sandy beach. According to the Maryland Historical Society, as many as twenty thousand people visited on a busy weekend, most of them arriving by a two-hour steamboat or ferry ride from Baltimore. The beach operated for eighty-five years, closing in 1962 when the amusement park was sold for development.

At least five other ideas were proposed, including one in 1918 that called for a double-decked bridge, but the 1929 stock market crash stopped those plans. World War II provided another stumbling block as all materials were being used in the war effort.

Finally, in 1947 the State Roads Commission was authorized to build a bridge that connected Annapolis to Kent Island. There were nay-sayers who thought the project foolhardy, believing the first bay winter would wipe out the bridge (the bay had frozen over in the winter of 1936, and would again in 1976–1977). Some referred to the bridge as Lane's Folly, after William Preston Lane Jr., the fifty-second governor of Maryland (1947–1951), who pushed for legislative approval to build the bridge.

Construction started in January 1949, and the two-lane Chesapeake Bay Bridge (not to be confused with the Chesapeake Bay Bridge Tunnel at the southern end of the bay that connects the two parts of Virginia) opened on July 30, 1952. It cost $45 million and at the time was the world's longest continuous over-water steel structure and the third-longest bridge in the world. The graceful curve was the product of efficiency more than aesthetics because the bridge had to be perpendicular to the shipping channel to avoid and prevent ships from running into the piers.

Where the ferries could carry at best 180 cars an hour, the bridge could handle nearly 4,000. Additionally, the ferries were at the mercy of the bay weather and north–south commercial freighter ship traffic. Although many were and are terrified of driving across the bridge, only the winds of Hurricane Isabel, in 2003, have caused the bridge to close to vehicular traffic.

The bridge was officially named posthumously on November 9, 1967, in honor of Governor Lane, who had passed away on February 7, 1967, at the age of seventy-four.

Work on the second, three-lane span started in 1960, opened on June 28, 1973, and cost $148 million. Each span measures about 4.3 miles with a peak vertical clearance of 186 feet above the bay. The two-lane span is primarily used for eastbound traffic and the three-lane for vehicles headed west. However, all lanes are reversible and when traffic is heavy, one lane on the three-lane bridge may be converted to eastbound.

Sixty years after the bay bridge opened, it's difficult to imagine what life was like without it. It's impossible to know what would have happened to the Eastern Shore if the bridges hadn't been built.

For those on the Western Shore, the bridge provided relatively painless access to the recreational facilities and beach towns along the Eastern Shore, including Ocean City in Maryland; Fenwick, Rehoboth, Bethany, and Lewes in Delaware; and Assateague and Chincoteague to the south. Within the past few years, development has blossomed in and around Cape Charles, Virginia, near the southern tip of the peninsula.

"The bridge made it easier to get to Baltimore and Washington," says former schoolteacher Judy Roberts of Lewes, Delaware, who is the daughter of a fourth-generation funeral director. "It also brought a lot more people to this area who have settled permanently or who have second homes. It changed our demographics, because a lot of people after they settled in wanted the same services they'd had where they used to live." Businesses moved in to meet this need, she says, pointing out the outlet stores that line Route 1, south of Lewes. On the other hand, "it's no longer the quiet little communities."

Additionally, as the livelihoods of many on the Eastern Shore came from agrarian and water-based harvests, the bridge meant they could ship their produce, poultry, fish, and other wares to the

Western Shore and other points west by land or to the Port of Baltimore for destinations around the country and the world.

On the negative side, the construction and upgrading of Route 50 bypassed the downtown area of Cambridge, causing the town center (and Dorchester County seat) to decline. A serious program has been undertaken to put stores back onto the main streets, some only temporary pop-up stores, to add to the admittedly fine restaurant options that have managed to succeed over the years. Additionally, a thriving arts community has emerged that always seems to be the harbinger of a more active and fulfilled downtown community.

Queen Anne's County has seen so much development, for both primary and secondary housing, and so many people commuting from the Eastern Shore to the other side, that the county has become part of the Washington, D.C. and Baltimore population center.

Since the bridge opened, traffic counts have increased annually. By 1953 there were about two million crossings and three million by 1957. It's now about twenty-four million a year. Officials figured it would take forty years to collect enough tolls to pay for the construction. Instead it took just ten. To avoid backups, which could be eighteen to twenty miles on the westbound side coming home after a nice weekend at the beach, the tollbooths were eliminated on that side and the price was doubled for those traveling eastbound. It's now $4 for a basic automobile and $1.50 for commuters, with an increase scheduled for 2013. As mentioned, some people are afraid to drive across the bridge. Although the state used to provide a driver for free (which really took two drivers, one to drive across and one to drive the first driver back), that service is now operated by a private company that charges about $25 to $30.

Another benefit of the bridge is revealed on the first Sunday in May, during the annual Bay Bridge Walk. Parking is provided and buses take pedestrians to the eastern end of the eastbound span and pick them up at the western end. A $1 donation for the bus ride helps defray the costs. A 10K is run earlier in the morning so the fifty thousand (annual average) walkers can stroll leisurely from one end to the other, taking time to examine expansion joints, enjoy views from the bridge that are a blur at fifty-five or more miles an hour, and learn about what they are seeing (e.g., the shipping channel). The walk was suggested by a Towson Boy Scout leader who wanted to know whether his troop could walk across the bridge while it was closed to vehicular traffic for maintenance. The first walk was held in 1975. It has been canceled a few times because of security concerns after September 11, 2001, heavy winds, and a recent bridge refurbishment. Many people who are terrified of driving across the bridge easily handle the gently-sloped walk. Water, toilets, and first-aid services are provided.

BALTIMORE INNER HARBOR

1954

Baltimore's harbor was already bustling by the early 1800s with ships arriving and departing from and to ports around the world. The port helped establish the town's strong industrial base and provided easy and pleasant passenger transportation along the Chesapeake Bay and to cities along the Atlantic Ocean. The destinations included the beaches on the Eastern Shore; Old Point, Norfolk, and Portsmouth in Virginia; Chesapeake Beach and Solomons in Maryland; and Washington, D.C. By the second decade of the twentieth century, streetcars and horse-drawn wagons moved along Light and Pratt Streets, which provided the edge of the watery basin.

Eventually, as in other cities, Baltimore's warehouses and wharfs became a dangerous place to work and the housing stock was in deplorable condition. One could almost imagine the rats in the middle of the twentieth century deserting what many now call Charm City.

By late 1954 and early 1955, a group of visionaries gathered as the Greater Baltimore Committee to work on the city's renaissance.

They started with the Charles Center Project, which included offices, a theater, and residences.

A master plan for the Inner Harbor was revealed in September 1964 that called for a science center, international trade center, housing, athletic fields, an esplanade, restaurants, theaters, shops, and a marina and boatel. The plans also included the completion and merging of Interstates 83 and 95. Some of these items made it to reality; others did not.

Behind this massive revitalization project were a group of elected officials and businesspeople, including J. Jefferson Miller, Isaac Hamburger, Thomas J. D'Alesandro Jr., Governor Theodore R. McKeldin, Barbara Johnson Bonnell, Martin Millspaugh, Morris Mechanic, Maryland Secretary of Transportation and future governor Harry Hughes, renowned architect Mies van der Rohe, Bernard Weissbourd, William Donald Schaefer (who served on the Baltimore city council from 1955 to 1971, then as mayor from 1971 to 1986, governor from 1987 to 1995, and finally as state comptroller from 1999 to 2007), innovative photographer Marion Warren, Hope Quackenbush, and Sandra (Sandy) Hillman.

James Wilson Rouse (who created the planned community of Columbia and the festival marketplace concept) was another driving force. Barbara Mikulski cut her political teeth on the campaign against the interstate highway cutting through and dividing Fells Point and went on to serve on the city council, as a member of Congress, and eventually (and still) in the US Senate. The list of people and companies involved in this historic urban renewal project continues.

A homesteading program started in the mid-1970s that allowed people to buy dilapidated town houses for $1 (and they were overpriced even at that rate). In exchange, they had to renovate the home within a time frame specified by whoever was selling it, the federal government or Baltimore.

By April 1973 a public wharf had been dedicated at the Inner Harbor and a year later construction began on the Inner Harbor promenade. This wide swath of parkland fronted the harbor and provided an open space where families could stroll, play ball, picnic, and attend public events. The Maryland Science Center opened in June 1976, and as part of the bicentennial celebration seven tall ships and a half-dozen military vessels from around the world came calling.

Many citizens objected to the Harborplace festival marketplace proposed by the Rouse Company plans because they'd become used to the open space, but it was approved by voter referendum in November 1978. Rouse broke ground two months later and in July 1980 the grand opening was celebrated.

The Rouse Company was involved in numerous other festival marketplace developments, including Faneuil Hall in Boston, South Street Seaport in New York, Bayside Marketplace in Miami, Market East in Philadelphia, and Riverwalk Marketplace in New Orleans. His criteria were rigid. The marketplace must have local (e.g., trolley) transportation between the market and local offices and hotels to serve as a visible reminder of the Inner Harbor complex and as a way to eliminate vehicular traffic jams; must have locally owned businesses rather than chain stores; and must have shops and restaurants that would draw locals during the winter, when the tourists were gone. Time has shown that where these components have been ignored or modified, the marketplace becomes just another mall and the attraction dwindles.

Representatives from Baltimore attended the 1980 convention of the National Association of Counties, with Prince George's County Councilmember Francis B. Francois as the outgoing president of the association, to invite a future convention to Baltimore. They promoted the city with a slogan along the lines of "If you haven't seen Baltimore in ten years, you haven't seen Baltimore." They were successful and in 1982, hundreds of elected county officials and staff members from around the country experienced the warmth and hospitality of a renovated and rejuvenated Baltimore. The association returned in 1987 and again in 1997, obviously impressed and pleased with the city's improvements.

One of the key visual components of the redevelopment deal was a building height maximum, which dictated that the buildings surrounding the Inner Harbor could be no more than ten stories to keep the area within a human scale visually. The only exception was the twenty-seven-story World Trade Center, designed by I. M. Pei's firm and becoming the tallest pentagonal building east of the Mississippi River.

Development continued, with the grand opening of the National Aquarium in Baltimore on August 8, 1981, drawing national media attention as then Governor Schaefer appeared in an old-time striped bathing outfit and went swimming with the seals as his part of a losing wager that the aquarium would not open on time and within budget.

By 1983 the beginning of the subway system was operational, and within another decade the light rail system was providing convenient and inexpensive transportation that made it easier to move around town and relieved traffic congestion and pollution.

By 1992 Oriole Park at Camden Yards (the first of the "retro" baseball parks to be constructed) had been built for the Baltimore Orioles baseball team and was the home stadium for the 1993 All-Star Game. In 1998 the new home for the Baltimore Ravens football team was open. The convention center has been enlarged, new hotels have been constructed, and continued growth is projected. The city has been home to numerous movies and two television series, *Homicide: Life on the Street* and *The Wire*. In late 2011 an HBO series, *VEEP,* starring Julia Louis-Dreyfus was filming episodes for its first season.

Under Schaefer's administration, the Baltimore City One Percent for Art ordinance (only the second in the country) was enacted, calling for funding of the arts and the creation of a citywide arts festival, ArtScape. The city is regularly recognized for its extraordinary appreciation and availability of public art.

Tall ships frequently visit and the Port of Baltimore is home to year-round cruise ship departures leaving for the Bahamas, Bermuda, New England and Canada, the Caribbean, and other ports. It's the fifth-busiest cruise port on the East Coast, with about 250,000 passengers taking advantage of its convenience and much that the city has to offer.

It took decades for Baltimore to reclaim its status as the major city that it is. Along the way the success of these projects has had a positive impact upon residents and nonresidents alike. Representatives from more than one hundred city and other governmental units were in touch with the Inner Harbor developers, taking away ideas and approaches to help make their projects successful. Six of them, including Sydney, Australia, and Barcelona, Spain, used the Baltimore model to restore and revitalize their harbor areas. According to the American Institute of Architects, the project is "one of the supreme achievements of large-scale urban design and development in US history," and in 2009 the Urban Land Institute cited the development as a model for waterfront development around the world.

Although Schaefer is credited as being the impetus behind these improvements, the initial spark was the meeting of minds and citizens to create that Greater Baltimore Committee.

READ'S DRUG STORE SIT-INS

On February 1, 1960, a sit-in occurred at the F. W. Woolworth store in Greensboro, North Carolina, and grabbed national attention. Sit-ins became a common way to protest segregation until blacks could sit anywhere on a bus, dine at any restaurant, and sit in any train station waiting room.

However, Greensboro's protest wasn't the start of the sit-in movement. As author Steve Ackerman has noted, Samuel Wilbert Tucker (1913–1990), an African-American attorney, led a sit-in in August 1939 in an Alexandria, Virginia, library, helping start the fight for equality.

Fifteen years later, on May 17, 1954, the US Supreme Court issued its decision on Brown v. Board of Education of Topeka, which said state segregation of schools was illegal. The civil rights movement finally had momentum in earnest.

A few months later, students from Morgan State College (now Morgan State University) had a spontaneous sit-in at the Read's drugstore lunch counter on January 20, 1955. The four-story Art

Deco building, constructed in 1933 and 1934 and displaying the slogan "Run Right to Read's," was at the corner of Howard and Lexington Streets. A small group of students waiting for the bus to take them to Morgan decided to go into Read's and sit at the lunch counter stools asking to be served. Although they could shop at the store, blacks weren't allowed to buy or consume food from the lunch counter, not even a cup of coffee or a glass of tea.

Although no one was arrested and no one was served, this almost thirty-minute demonstration was followed by sit-ins at other Read's stores; sometimes light-skinned students who often "passed" (as white) would see whether they would be served. Within a month the management at the chain's headquarters said all thirty-seven of its Baltimore-area stores would serve both black and white people. Other businesses, including a movie theater and an ice cream shop, were the subject of sit-ins, but these events weren't aimed at the media and they received relatively little news coverage. There are few pictures or film clips of the first event. Read's eventually was purchased by the Rite Aid chain, and the Howard Street store was closed. Although it went through some renovations, it eventually was abandoned, purchased by the city, and allowed to deteriorate, and all of the interior furnishings, including the lunch counter and stools, are long gone.

Read's had great company during its heyday, with the flagship locations for four department stores in the busy downtown shopping spot. The oldest one was Hutzler's Brothers Company, which was started in 1858. At its prime, Hutzler's occupied 325,000 square feet and allowed blacks to shop there. Another institution was Hecht's Department Store, which became part of the May Company, with a history dating back to 1857. In 1881 Posner's—which would become Stewart's in 1901—arrived and became the toniest place to shop. Hochschild-Kohn, or more familiarly Hochschild's, became the fourth of the downtown stores. With World War II, race riots, and the move to the suburbs, the department stores moved and died, all long gone (except for the May Company) before the turn of the twenty-first century.

Although some people have forgotten, the Baltimore Read's Drug Store sit-in was not the first peaceful demonstration of this time. What is considered the first lunch counter sit-ins for the civil rights movement probably took place in July 1958 in Wichita, Kansas, and about a month later in Oklahoma City, Oklahoma. Both drugstores were integrated within the month. Another noteworthy 1960 demonstration took place in Nashville, Tennessee. Other peaceful demonstrations had taken place around the globe for different reasons, but not at luncheon counters.

More noise was made in 2010 as Morgan students and others started protesting again because the company that bought the original Read's building (and others) planned to tear it down as part of the $150 million area Lexington Square redevelopment plan in what is called the Superblock in Baltimore's west side. As noted, nothing of the original store—particularly the lunch counter or the stools—remained in the building. Preservationists, civil rights leaders, and historians wanted at least the facade saved and incorporated into the design.

City and state agencies held public hearings, the destruction and preservation issues were discussed on local talk shows, tours of the block were given by Baltimore Heritage (a preservation organization), and a panel discussed it at the Reginald F. Lewis Museum of Maryland African American History and Culture. And, once again, students (this time from City Neighbors Charter School) protested as a class project on peaceful civil disobedience.

In defense of the Dawson Company (the lead developer of Lexington Square), since 2006, when the company started working on the project, Dawson has worked with the Maryland Historic Trust to identify historic buildings and apparently no one mentioned the historic sit-ins at Read's Drug Store. Dawson officials say they didn't know the building's history until the current protests started. To refute any charge that they're guilty of prejudicial behavior, Dawson Company officials note that it is a second-generation African-American-owned firm whose founder, Harold Dawson Sr., broke the color barrier in Atlanta. Previously the Dawson Company also redeveloped the Centerpoint apartment complex, also on Baltimore's west side. Among the proposals for that specific space is a working pharmacy, perhaps staffed by the pharmacy school students from the University of Maryland or the College of Notre Dame—an idea from Joe Nattans, grandson of the former owner. He also suggested an exhibit of site-specific objects. Others have suggested that the exhibits be located at the Lewis museum, the Morgan campus, or the Great Blacks in Wax Museum.

On April 28, 2011, John Majors, executive vice president of the Dawson Company, proposed to the Baltimore Commission for Historical and Architectural Preservation an on-site exhibit that will honor the Morgan students, their accomplishment, and their place in history. The plan is said to contain 300,000 square feet of residential space in 300 units, 178,000 square feet of retail space on the ground and second floors, and a 120-room hotel while saving the north and west facades of the building.

Just as the Read's sit-in in 1955 showed the effectiveness of peaceful demonstrations and set the tone for the civil rights battles that would be staged in the 1960s, the protests of this decade have proven successful in obtaining a balance between yesteryear and the future.

SOPHIE KERR PRIZE

1965

Since Sophie Kerr died in 1965, she has helped countless people in ways she could probably never imagine. Born in Denton, in Caroline County, she went to Hood College in Frederick and then earned a master's degree from the University of Vermont. She left small-town life for Pittsburgh and then moved to New York, where she became a magazine managing editor. She became a prolific writer whose articles appeared in such magazines as *Saturday Evening Post, McCall's,* and *Collier's Saturday Review of Literature.* She wrote about intelligent, determined women who pulled themselves up by the bootstraps and succeeded against all odds, because she was one herself.

Nationally renowned and hitting her peak popularity in the 1930s and 1940s, Kerr wrote more than five hundred short stories, twenty-three novels, numerous magazine articles, and some poetry. Several of her stories were made into television shows or episodes and movies. One, "Chin-Chin," was made into a Broadway play and then two movies, *Big Hearted Herbert* in 1934 and *Father Is a Prince* in 1940. As recently as 1955, one of her stories made it onto the live hourly television anthology show *Matinee Theatre*.

You can find a few of her works at the Enoch Pratt library and several more if you stop by the Caroline County library. Each library has a couple of copies of *Sound of Petticoats and Other Stories of the Eastern Shore*. Amazon sells her books, ranging from a Kindle version for $1 to hardcover copies for a few dollars to more than $100. Tom Martin of Bookplate, a Chestertown bookstore, says he generally has a whole slew of them, including paperbacks, hardbacks, books with dust jackets and without, some signed and some not. James Dawson, owner of Unicorn Bookshop on Route 50 in Trappe, says he occasionally receives a copy of one of her books or a request for one.

In her will, Kerr left a $578,000 endowment to Washington College in Chestertown, Kent County, about thirty miles as the crow flies from her hometown. The college was established in 1782 as a private independent liberal arts school. It was the tenth college founded in the United States and the first after the country's fight for independence. George Washington gave his permission to use his name, served on the Board of Visitors and Governors, and contributed to its founding. It became coeducational in 1891. The small, private, rural liberal arts institution on Maryland's Eastern Shore has a student population of about 1,300 undergraduates and 100 postgraduates. Many are drawn to it because of the bucolic setting within close range of boating water while still being only a couple of hours from Washington, D.C., Baltimore, Annapolis, and the Atlantic Ocean beaches of Maryland and Delaware. The school is close to everywhere and near nowhere.

The provisions in Kerr's will stated that half of the fund's income would provide for an annual literary prize for the graduating senior showing the most promise as a writer. The student doesn't have to be an English or literature major and doesn't have to promise to go into either of those fields. That prize has ranged from $9,000 to nearly $70,000 since it was first awarded in 1968. It is the nation's largest undergraduate literary prize and over the years has totaled more than $1.4 million.

Another portion of the endowment's income funds scholarships that include four-year $1,500 tuition scholarships to an entering student who intends to major in English. Still another part of her fund goes to student publications, library purchases, and other literary activities. It has attracted other literary-minded grants and donations from the National Endowment for the Humanities and from alumna Betty Brown Casey, who donated the funds for the O'Neill House, where writers and creative minds gather for intellectual and collegial stimulation and support.

A list of some of the alumni indicates the quality of the student body and their potential. Among the notables are John Emory (Emory University), Colonel Hiram Staunton Brown (president of RKO movie studios), James M. Cain (author of *The Postman Always Rings Twice, Mildred Pierce,* and *Double Indemnity*) while his father was president of the college, and Louis L. Goldstein (former comptroller of Maryland).

The significance and attraction of the prize draws students who want to study English and literature from almost every state and a couple dozen foreign countries. Students wishing to be considered for the prize may submit creative nonfiction, fiction, poetry, essays, blogs, stage plays, and other forms of creative expression. The writers' union tends to be the largest student organization on the campus.

Yet, it's what happens with the rest of the income from the endowment that merits Paul Harvey, "rest of the story" coverage.

The school is noted for its lecture series, also funded by the Kerr endowment, that attracts famed writers, editors, scholars, and other notables. They travel to Chestertown, with its five thousand or so population, to lecture and talk with students, staff, faculty, area residents, and visitors. Anyone and everyone may attend, no fee charged.

Natasha Trethewey, the 2007 Pulitzer Prize recipient for *Native Guard,* was the featured speaker for the 2011 Sophie Kerr Weekend. This annual event, sponsored through the Kerr funds, brings high school writers to the campus to experience the literary life through workshops, lectures, and other arts events.

Over the 2010–2011 academic year, a typically eclectic group of speakers shared their ideas with the students and outsiders. Colum McCann, the 2011 recipient of the International IMPAC Award, has visited the campus twice and was the keynote speaker for the 2011 Kerr Prize. Fashion designer Andrae Gonzalo, star of Bravo TV's *Project Runway,* brought his new line to the school as he shared the podium with Harvard University Professor Stephen Burt, author of *Poetry and Project Runway: Should Book Critics Take Their Cues from Tim Gunn?*

Since the Kerr Prize was established, the speaker list has included Edward Albee, Joseph Brodsky, Gwendolyn Brooks, Lucille Clifton, Mary Karr, Toni Morrison, Katherine Ann Porter, Joyce Carol Oates, Robert Pinskey, and Jane Smiley. These speakers provide the inspiration and bolster the drive for the next generation of American writers.

The 2011 prize, for $61,062 (about double the average salary a liberal arts major might earn in his or her first year out in the real world), went to Lisa Jones, an anthropology major. Each May, around the time the prize is awarded, someone writes an article about previous winners. Most seem to delight in a snarky gloat that "no one's made it" or "some seem to look upon the prize as a curse."

Kay MacIntosh, director of media relations for Washington College, quickly (and perhaps a little on the understandably self-defensive side) responds, "To the contrary, most of our winners have gone on to use their writing skills in the workplace, some have published books, and others are working as professors, editors, or marketing executives." Periodically the college updates its "Where Are They Now?" list to confirm the prize's intangible and financial value.

Among the recipients, Unicorn bookstore owner Dawson notes that William L. Thompson, 1970 Sophie Kerr Prize winner and a former *Baltimore Sun* reporter, has written a number of nonfiction books about the Eastern Shore and the Chesapeake Bay, and a novel set on the Eastern Shore, *The Waterbusher*. Thompson ponders the source of a person's posterity: "Today, we only think of Alfred Nobel because he established the Nobel Peace Prize. Few remember that he got his money by inventing dynamite."

All of this is from a small-town woman who, with a few strokes of her pen upon a will, left more legacy than all her works combined.

WESTERNPORT FLOOD MITIGATION PROJECT

1996

Whether it's rain, rapid snowmelt, or a hurricane, we've heard a lot about the Mississippi, Missouri, James (Virginia), Mouse (North Dakota), and other rivers overtopping their banks and causing millions of dollars in lost habitat and crops. Despite permanent and emergency levees, sandbags, and other attempts to keep Mother Nature's wrath from the front door, basement, and attic, the floods continue. In some cases, levees broke or dam spillways—built to control flooding—were opened to divert raging waters from highly populated to lesser populated towns and cities, all in hopes of preventing nearly incalculable damage.

Property owners receive suggestions or mandates that they should or must buy flood insurance, but no amount of money can replace family photos and heirlooms. No monetary value can be placed on a souvenir or keepsake, even some silly souvenir from a long-ago vacation or special event. Requiring homes be built on stilts within hundred-year flood plains has not proven totally successful either.

In response to our finally awakening to the damages done by draining, damming, rerouting, and otherwise interfering with Mother Nature's design, flood mitigation programs have been implemented in some places. Towns in low-lying areas along rivers have been razed or homes and businesses have been moved and located on higher grounds. Now, rather than trying to prevent damage from hundred-year-storms and floods that seem to come more frequently than every one hundred years, governments and their populations are eliminating the potential of damage and heartbreak.

Thus is the case with Westernport, Maryland, in Allegany County, a small town whose nonnative history dates from 1758. In area it is less than one square mile, and it's located where the Georges Creek, basically paralleling Route 36, empties into the North Branch of the Potomac River. When it was named, it was the river's westernmost navigable town and ships carried cut timber and coal downriver to the Washington, D.C., area. As of the 2000 census, Westernport had a population of 2,104.

The town had suffered from flooding before, and it happened again early in January 1996 due to an early heavy snowmelt. It was mild, though, compared to what would come nine months later when Hurricane Fran, reaching a category 3 rating on the Saffir-Simpson Hurricane Scale, visited the area. The storm formed off the coast of Africa near the Cape Verde Islands on August 23 and took until September 8 to dissipate off the northeastern coast of Canada. The storm made landfall near Cape Fear, North Carolina, and tore a northwest path up the East Coast through Virginia and then into western Maryland. It was blamed for thirty-seven deaths (none in Maryland) and $5 billion ($100 million in Maryland) in damage, in 1966 dollars. The name Fran was removed from the list of future hurricanes, replaced by the name Fay.

By the time Fran reached Maryland, it had been downgraded to a tropical storm, but the slow forward movement allowed it to dump six inches of rain that produced severe flash flooding in some areas and prolonged flooding in others. On September 22 Georges Creek overflowed its streambed into Westernport, flooding Main Street and damaging dozens of homes and businesses. The flooding in Frederick, Garrett, Allegany, and Washington Counties was severe enough to warrant a presidential disaster declaration.

The governor convened a flood mitigation task force to recommend ways to minimize or eliminate future flooding. Relying on suggestions from the Federal Emergency Management Agency (FEMA), the Maryland Emergency Management Agency, and the Association of State Floodplain Managers, the committee considered methods to address the flooding problems. They also heard from individual county public works departments, the Maryland State Highway Administration, the Natural Resources Conservation Service, and the US Army Corps of Engineers.

The initial report was released on January 31, 1997, and included such routine maintenance and restoration projects as removing debris from the rivers; stabilizing streambeds; and repairing utilities, bridges, and structures. Additional funding was made available for long-term projects in nearby Lonaconing and Locust Grove.

More extensive work was recommended for Westernport. In all, about three hundred buildings in the hundred-year flood plain and two dozen more in the five hundred–year flood plain were purchased and removed.

According to a report by J. J. Prats of Springfield, Virginia, to the Historical Marker Database (www.hmdb.org), twenty-seven homes in Westernport were removed from the hundred-year flood plain and other infrastructure repairs and remodeling were accomplished. A major objective in preventing future flooding was to incorporate "non-structural alternatives in their flood recovery efforts."

The first phase included the home removal, "reconstruction of streambank retaining walls to protect highway infrastructure, repair and relocation of sanitary sewers, and the environmental restoration and re-establishment of the floodplain area for a one-mile stretch of Georges Creek." Additionally, the creek channel was realigned and stabilized, with improved bank sloping.

Phase two established Creekside Park in the flood plain open space. With input from students, educators, senior citizens, property owners, business and civic organizations, community leaders, and elected officials, the design called for numerous entertainment, relaxation, and educational opportunities. The green space is part of a dream that will create a trail and greenway system along Georges Creek from its headwaters in Frostburg, Maryland, in a south by southwest direction through Lonaconing, Moscow, and Barton to the Potomac River in Westernport.

Prats further reported that vegetation was planted along the stream banks to help slow the river flow, which would:

- Decrease erosion in town and downstream

- Create pools that would improve fish habitat

- Shade the habitat to help maintain the water temperature

- Allow the waterway to stabilize itself

As with other areas in the country, development had tried to overrule nature and the creek and its tributaries had been straightened, dredged, and encroached upon. Steps to correct these "corrections" continue to be taken.

A historic marker about the 1996 flood has been erected and a stone marker on Main Street (Maryland Route 937) was dedicated to those who lost their homes to Tropical Storm Fran and the flood waters.

Unusual spring snowstorms, one or two days of continuous rain, and a late or sudden snowmelt can still cause rising water levels that overflow river and creek banks and put enough water into a basement that the local volunteer fire department has to pump it out. And periodically personnel from Westernport Elementary School have to move materials from the floor and lower shelves to higher ones. The school had flood shields for the windows and doors installed in 1990, but when the 1996 flood occurred, the seals had not been maintained and had deteriorated, so the school suffered major damage. In some places boards may be placed over windows, not to prevent water seeping in, but to prevent debris from hitting and breaking the windows. Flood plain designation maps continue to be altered, shifting an inch or two this way or a foot that way as Mother Nature changes the ins and outs of the waterways.

Whatever the damage, the changes that have taken place since the floods of January and September 1996 have materially abated flood damage potential to Westernport. And since the creation of Creekside Park, with the Biggs Pavilion, numerous events have been held there, including the town's sesquicentennial celebration, with vendors, arts and crafts, food booths, hay rides, entertainment, pie-baking and vegetable-eating contests, and other activities. The annual Homefest celebrates the joy of the town's existence with food, activities, and entertainment on the Creekside stage. For the moment, they do not perform a rain dance.

TOBACCO BUYOUT

2000

Tobacco was a cash crop in Maryland for nearly 370 years. State and other jurisdictional currencies could fluctuate in value on little more than a whim, but for the most part, tobacco was steady. It was also a labor-intensive crop, taking about 250 backbreaking man hours per acre. A farmer was lucky to be able to grow ten acres per person working the crop. It has to be planted indoors, transplanted outdoors, harvested, and then wrapped into "hands" and placed in tobacco barns to be air-cured for nine months. Less labor-intensive crops can be raised with as little as four hours of work per acre.

Nevertheless, the crop remained the economic linchpin until late into the twentieth century, with its value placed at about two-thirds of all agriculture production in the area as late as 1992. That started to change in the early 1980s when a drought adversely affected this crop's quantity and quality because it is particular about the weather. Auction prices plummeted and never really returned to the previous level, while the cost of growing the crop kept increasing.

On the other hand, the suburbs of Washington, D.C., were slowly (and sometimes rapidly) and inexorably buying up open fields at prices that far exceeded the monies earned from tobacco. By 2010 the average age of a Maryland tobacco farmer was seventy-two and the younger generation was not interested in perpetuating the family tradition.

Primarily raised in Calvert, Charles, and St. Mary's Counties, tobacco also was grown in Prince George's and Anne Arundel Counties. (It was grown for a short time on the Eastern Shore but very quickly replaced with other crops.) Taking a short drive out of the city, you soon would be looking at acres and acres of tobacco plants, tobacco barns with their side flaps open so the air could circulate while it cured the tobacco, and eight tobacco auction houses in Hughesville, Upper Marlboro, and Waldorf. Tobacco was such a dominant part of Calvert County life that the county flag (designed by Mrs. Robert M. Coffin and adopted in 1966) and seal feature a tobacco leaf.

Then, in November 1998 the Tobacco Master Settlement Agreement was reached between tobacco companies and the attorneys general of forty-six states, including Maryland. Our portion amounted to $4.5 billion and the powers that be decided to fund the Maryland Tobacco Crop Conversion Program or buyout. Part of that included providing guidance for the farmers as they determined the most productive and profitable use of their land. Maryland was the only state to provide this type of incentive to not grow tobacco. North Carolina, which grows more tobacco than any other state, used the settlement money to foster foreign-country markets.

Maryland's buyout, agreed upon in 1999, gave the growers 5 percent of the tobacco payout if the farmers would agree to stop growing tobacco and participating in its growth or sale. The rest of the money was earmarked for medical research and programs to convince people not to start smoking or to help smokers stop. Based on an average of the total number of pounds of tobacco grown in each year between 1996 and 1998, the grower would receive a dollar per pound for each of the next ten years. They had a five-year period, from 2000 to 2004, to sign up, and eventually 92 percent (854 growers) of the producers agreed, taking nearly eight million pounds of tobacco out of the market. The others are Amish, who do not approve of receiving government handouts, or independent farmers who wanted to stay in the tobacco business.

The payout started in 2001 and will last through 2015, with the tenth year of the first payouts taking place in 2011.

Part of the agreement was the grower had to consent to keep the land in agriculture production, meaning it could not be sold for housing or commercial development. Additionally, the farmer received a 10 percent decrease in the county and state easement valuation. What to do with the land was the next decision. Some farmers already had greenhouses and started using them for flowers to be sold locally or through grocery stores. Others grow Christmas trees (although it takes twelve to fifteen years to grow marketable trees), vegetables (bok choy, tomatoes, peppers, cucumbers, wheat, green beans, and numerous herbs), hay, soybeans, pick-it-yourself crops (raspberries, blueberries, and strawberries), corn that's sold to Perdue for chicken feed, goats for meat to sell to the growing East Coast Muslim population, and other livestock.

One problem that appeared with the increased availability of local, farm-raised meats was the lack of a slaughtering and processing plant within the five-county area. No one has expressed an interest in establishing such a service here, so the Southern Maryland Agricultural Development Commission provided funds for two meat "freezer trailers" to transport the slaughtered and processed meat to the farm or to retail stores.

According Dr. Christine L. Bergmark, executive director of the commission, in the 2010 year-end report, the St. Mary's Cooperative Extension and University of Maryland trial of growing catnip (a member of the mint family) is nearly complete. It showed that "this core product in the pet industry is very profitable on a per acre basis with several high profit derivative products associated with it and could be a potent option for former Maryland tobacco farmers, utilizing redundant tobacco barns and modified general farm equipment for harvesting and drying."

Several properties have been converted to help develop an equine community. An Equine Guide lists sixty-four horse farms and associated services, including twenty-three equine hay-producing farms. It also lists farriers, veterinary and health care services, tack shops, feed mills, equine associations, and local riding trails.

According to Connie and Gerald Byrne, former tobacco growers who had abandoned tobacco before the buyout, they and seventeen other grape growers have formed the Port of Leonardtown Winery, which coordinates activities, purchases equipment, staffs a tasting room, participates in festivals, and markets the wine. In a report filed online with a wine industry site, farmers also have created a Southern Maryland Wine Growers Cooperative. Winemaking is still a young industry in this part of the state, so designating one place as a winery relieves a lot of financial burden on farmers still trying to determine which grapes thrive the best and produce a good wine. The cooperative helps them pool production and marketing resources. So far, Vidal Blanc, Viognier, Barbera, and Petit Verdot seem to be the most amenable to the local climate and soil. Their first harvest was crushed in 2009 and the winery, located in an abandoned state highway administration building, was open for tours and tastings. The wines are good enough to have won a couple of medals in an Atlantic Seaboard competition.

Tobacco barns are slatted to allow air through to help dry the tobacco and are not insulated, so the question of what to do with them is still being addressed on several levels. Preservationists don't want them to disappear. In some cases they're being used for boat storage; one barn is now the visitor center at Calvert Cliffs State Park; and a tobacco museum has been established in another.

Joyce Stinnett Baki, tourism specialist with the Calvert County Department of Economic Development, says a new attraction opened in three phases over 2011 and 2012, starting with "a produce cooperative where farmers bring their produce or other farm items that are sold at the farm stand off Route 231 at Spider Hall Farm. Everything sold is grown or made in Maryland, including produce, cheese, ice cream, meats, seafood, and a few crafts."

By the fall of 2011, says Baki, "the farm had an educational facility that allows schoolchildren (and adult groups) to visit a working farm. In September and October there is a corn maze, hayrides, and pumpkin patch." A farm museum is scheduled to open in spring 2012. "The family that runs Spider Hall is a farming family that has been there for generations. Susan Cox and her daughter Catherine are also educators, so they have developed curriculum for the program."

Additionally, says Baki, a "farm stay" program opened in 2011 where "you can stay—for a weekend or a week—at a farmhouse and you'll be able to assist with the farming or just relax."

All this from a crop that was grown just so it could go up in smoke.

IF YOU CAN'T DEFEAT 'EM, EAT 'EM

2002

In 1962 commercial growers and marketers of the Chinese gooseberry changed the fuzzy-skinned fruit's name to kiwifruit or kiwi because the original name just didn't have any zing to it. The sale and consumption of the northern Chinese snakehead fish (*Channa argus*) might benefit from a similar marketing gimmick. Admittedly it's a tasty fish, it's seriously ugly, with a lot of nasty teeth, has a terrible reputation, and anyone catching one of these fish must destroy it one way or another.

Most Americans became familiar with this invasive species a month or so after an angler caught an adult snakehead on May 18, 2002, in a little pond behind the Crofton, Maryland, post office (not Lake Louise at the Route 3 entrance to Crofton). It was eventually determined that someone had dumped the adult fish in the pond (referred to on some online maps as Walking Fish Pond) in 2000, and because the statute of limitations is two years, the man who dumped them was not charged. Apparently he paid less than $40 for the pair and the fine would have been $40.

By October 2002 the US Fish and Wildlife Service had banned all snakeheads from importation and interstate transportation. You cannot take, possess, transport, sell, purchase, barter, export, or import the snakeheads—including their eggs.

These fish have no natural predators in the United States, breed in large numbers (females produce as many as 100,000 eggs a year), live as long as eight years, and have voracious appetites. Put mildly, they are considered undesirable.

Although it's not known for sure whether any of the fish had escaped to the nearby Little Patuxent River prior to their "discovery" in Crofton (the fish can wriggle across land), natural resources people tried to destroy them before they made their way southeast toward the Chesapeake Bay. Among other things, the Department of Natural Resources built a berm of sandbags and silt fences around the pond to make sure there was no water overflow or wriggling fish escaping to the nearby river. Biologists tried catching the fish by dip-netting them, but that was effective only on larger fish. They applied herbicides and rotenone (pesticide); the rotenone worked, but it also killed other native fishes living in the pond. The state eventually drained the pond. After all was said and done, more than 1,200 snakeheads were recovered. Including providing personnel, establishing a panel to deal with the problem, and pursuing eradication efforts, the costs ran an estimated $110,000.

These weren't the first snakeheads captured in the country, for they'd been found in San Bernardino, California, in 1997, the St. Johns River in Florida in 2001, and in Worcester County, Massachusetts, in 2001. They originated and are popular in China, Russia, and North and South Korea. The fish lives in freshwater and does not like cold weather, so officials thought it could not survive winter in the Maryland area—but they were wrong.

A few of the fish had been sold in pet or aquarium stores, but most of them came from Asian live-fish markets.

After the Crofton fish were destroyed, others (not genetically related to the Crofton fish) were found in Potomac River tributaries (particularly on the Virginia side of the river) and officials feared they would overtake the bass that are such a moneymaker for Charles County (more than one hundred bass-fishing contests take place every year) and other Maryland jurisdictions. Of course, the bass were a foreign species when thirty-five of them were introduced in 1854. Instead, the snakeheads seem to have settled on a diet of crappies, and they have been known to dine on crustaceans, insects and worms, snakes, frogs, tadpoles, and small birds.

One way of making sure they don't survive to produce more snakeheads is to eat them. Supposedly they have a light, clean taste because they are freshwater fish. They will go into slightly brackish water along the Chesapeake and down the Potomac, but not too far. Several prominent chefs have included them in their menus, including Bryan Voltaggio (Volt in Frederick), Spike Gjerde (Woodberry Kitchen), Scott Drewno (Washington's The Source by Wolfgang Puck), and Chad Wells (Alewife Baltimore). Although the Maryland Department of Natural Resources is said to be promoting this idea, detractors think people should not be given an incentive to raise the snakeheads so they can be caught and sold to the restaurant and home kitchen market.

The fish aren't plentiful enough (yet) and they've been hiding and nesting in shallow waters where commercial fishing boats can't venture. That means commercial fishermen are not taking them as a main catch, so they aren't always available. Usually they're a by-catch with a net full of other fish, usually catfish. Wells has been particularly active in promoting the fish at such special events as the Maryland Seafood Festival and a snakehead fishing competition (not a catch-and-release operation). The casual angler who snags a snakehead should cook whatever is caught before eating it because you don't always know whether bacteria or parasites are present in the water where the fish was caught, Wells says, the snakehead should not be served raw as sushi.

One unintentional revenue stream was the making of low-budget, derivative films by independent movie makers about this invasive species. The first film, *Snakehead Terror* (2004), starred Bruce Boxleitner (that should be enough explanation), Carol Alt, and Chelan Simmons in a truly horror-filled concept that officials in a small, down-on-its-heels town throws human growth hormones into the local lake to help the invasive snakeheads grow and revive the defunct fishing industry. Of course, the fish show their gratitude by consuming everything in sight: animal, vegetable, or human (oh, that is animal—right). The tagline was "The fish are really biting." Although it wasn't classified as a humorous film, snow-covered mountains are shown as the backdrop of the Crofton pond. Yes, Maryland has mountains, but they can't be seen from this Anne Arundel town that's large enough for only one zip code.

A second film, *Frankenfish* (also 2004), starred Tory Kittles, K. D. Aubert, and China Chow, who investigate a wealthy hunter who has genetically altered the fish to attack and kill local residents. It was classified under the categories of action, comedy, and horror and had a tagline of "Welcome to the bottom of the food chain."

Obviously the growth of the northern snakehead can't be blamed on one poor guy who dumped a couple of fish in a pond behind a post office. However, he may want to keep the event a secret from his children and grandchildren.

MALLOWS BAY GHOST FLEET

2010

About thirty miles south of Washington, on the Maryland shore of the Potomac River, is the quiet Mallows Bay in an equally quiet part of Charles County near Nanjemoy. The 185-acre Mallows Bay Park surrounding it provides exceptional outdoor recreation options including fishing, hiking, a kayak launch, a fifty-foot timber boarding pier, and a concrete boat launch. It's a fairly new park, formally opened on September 29, 2010, by officials from the county and the Maryland Department of Natural Resources, the governmental bodies that funded the facility. It also has car and boat trailer parking.

Until the park opened, getting to Mallows Bay involved putting a boat in the water in Virginia and finding your way across the wide Potomac or somewhere north or south of the bay and paddling or motoring into the shallow waters. Now it's part of the Potomac River Paddle Trail.

During emergencies, visitors might see the local fire and rescue teams heading into the river, but the emergency unit has its own boat ramp. Other than having some osprey chatter at you if you venture too close to their nest, some heron taking flight just as you've framed the perfect picture, or a couple of mature and immature bald eagles playing tag with a freshly caught fish, the emergency responses are about the only thing exciting that happens in Mallows Bay.

To find the real treasure of this area, unlike any other park in the state, area, or country, you have to look down and around you, in between and beneath the little islands of short brush and trees. For there, and the reason you want to go during low tide and take a shallow draw, flat-bottomed boat rather than a sailboat or V-hulled motorboat into the area, are the remains of dozens of sunken ships. This is the Ghost Fleet of Mallows Bay, said to be the largest collection of sunken wooden ships in the Western Hemisphere and maybe the world.

The story behind this fleet started about one hundred years ago and is a favorite tale told often by Donald G. Shomette, author of the *Ghost Fleet of Mallows Bay* (Schiffer Publishing, 1996) and the acknowledged expert in this field.

As Shomette tells it, President Woodrow Wilson started rallying the country to begin gearing up for World War I in early April 1917. Europe had been battling the Germans for more than two years and the German submarine attacks were a danger to everything that sailed the Atlantic. This sudden shift into high gear was more than a mind-change situation. Since the turn of the twentieth century we had launched only a little more than 500,000 tons of ocean-worthy ships and now we needed to construct six million tons in a year and a half.

It would be almost two years before Frederick Eustis, an engineer, proposed a different approach to William Denman, chair of the US Shipping Board. Instead of building expensive steel vessels, Eustis proposed a fleet of wooden ships. The lumber, yellow pine or Douglas fir, was readily available and cost less, and production could be accomplished by companies other than the shipyards involved in producing other naval products. They could also be manufactured faster than the U-boats were sinking ships, Eustis said. The plan called for a thousand coal-burning steamships to be built within eighteen months. Ships were designed to be standardized, between 240 and 300 feet long, and carry an average of 3,500 tons of cargo. In perhaps the biggest prefabrication project of its time, all the wooden parts were precut, numbered, finished to specifications, and then shipped to eighty-seven building yards around the country. Schools were opened to train the necessary personnel.

George W. Goethals, the man who finally built the Panama Canal, was the general manager. Within five months, though, as the orders for wood stock were being placed, Goethals and Denman were in a power struggle, complicated by political infighting, and the project looked as though it might sink the flotilla before the Germans had a chance.

The project continued in fits and starts, with the first wooden bottom finally launched on December 1, 1917, in the Pacific. A year later only 134 had been finished, while 263 more were less than halfway completed. When the Germans surrendered in November, none of the ships had crossed the Atlantic.

Perhaps that was good, because an ensuing Senate investigation charged that the ships were "badly designed, weakly constructed, poorly caulked, leaked excessively, and were too small and expensive for long-distance cargo hauling," says Shomette.

For one thing, the ships had to carry too much coal to fuel the transatlantic journey to allow much room or tonnage for cargo. By the time diesel-fueled ships came onto the market, making these wooden ships obsolete before they were launched, 265 of them had been placed in operation. The postwar economic downturn put another nail into the wooden coffin.

The question then became what to do with them. The ships were gathered in the James River in Virginia and kept afloat at the staggering cost of $50,000 a month. They were put on the market "as is and where is."

Western Marine and Salvage Company (WM&SC) bought most of the ships for $750,000 and hauled them to the Potomac in an area off Widewater, Virginia. They would take each ship to Alexandria to have the machinery removed, the ship burned to release the metal fittings, and then disposed of in a nearby marsh, covered with dredge spoil. One problem after another plagued the operation and local fisherman complained that Widewater was too valuable for its shad and herring to be part of this operation. Eventually WM&SC was convinced or persuaded to move its operation across the river to a 566-acre farm around Mallows Bay.

Amid public controversy from Maryland watermen, the invasion of Mallows Bay began early November 7, 1925, and the first thirty-one ships were burned, their skeletons hauled into the bay, and the destruction process started in earnest. Of course, this venture didn't fare much better and within four years, after WM&SC had brought 169 ships to this ghost fleet hangout, the profits from metal salvage and the stock market crash started the final sinking of WM&SC. The company filed for bankruptcy in March 1931.

The ships weren't totally idle, says Shomette, for within three years, dozens of independent scrap salvagers (salvors) were combing the ships for metal and "at least five floating brothels and no fewer than 26 illegal stills were reportedly erected nearby."

World War II changed all that. Bethlehem Steel was hired to recover the estimated twenty thousand tons of iron from the remaining 110 ships still in the bay. They abandoned the project in late 1944 with one hundred ships still sitting in Mallows Bay.

The next rallying cry came in 1963, when watermen and a company called Idamont, along with the US Army Corps of Engineers, started working toward another destruction and removal effort.

Progress on paper was going great guns until 1968, when congressional hearings disclosed that the company was really an arm of Potomac Electric Power Company trying to acquire nearby Sandy Point for a generating plant without going through the maze of public and stockholder disclosures.

A strange thing happened in the process of exploring these violations against the Securities and Exchange Commission. The Chesapeake Biological Laboratory, the National Audubon Society, and the Department of the Interior stated the decaying wrecks had become their own ecosystem and removing them would upset the new balance of nature and the wildlife they supported and cause irreparable pollution. The fleet was left alone—again.

Fast-forward to 1993, when a Maryland grant approved the cataloging and archaeological documentation of what was there. The survey indicated there were eighty-eight wooden Emergency Fleet Corporation ships; other wrecks, barges, canoes, and workboats; and even a car ferry named the *Accomac*. The ships have provided the same safe harbor as ships that are deliberately sunk today.

Finally, after more than a decade of work by Charles County's parks and recreation division, led by Tom Roland, the bay no longer collects the unwanted relics of the past. Instead the bay's sunken hulks have created a future for us to enjoy with tranquility and enjoyment of nature and a way to explore a brief and convoluted few moments of naval history.

PLUCKY CHICKENS

2011

Raising chickens, particularly on the Eastern Shore, is big business. The Delmarva (DELaware, MARyland, and VirginiA) chicken industry started in 1923 and has grown into a $2 billion annual industry, of which about 45 percent is from Maryland, another 45 percent is from Delaware, and the rest is from Virginia. Chickens accounted for about 40 percent of Maryland's cash farm income in 2009. With 15,000 people employed in the four chicken production companies and 1,700 chicken farmers, the poultry business and tourism are the two main industries on the Eastern Shore.

The United States is the second largest producer of chickens, after Brazil, and Delmarva is about the sixth-largest market within the United States, producing 3.42 million pounds of poultry in 2010. Maryland alone is eighth in the country. Most of the grain grown on Maryland's Eastern Shore is used for chicken feed. According to the Delmarva Poultry Industry Inc., each job in the poultry processing industry creates 7.2 jobs elsewhere. A University of Maryland study concluded that "jobs directly and indirectly dependent upon the broiler chicken industry represent over one out of every twelve jobs in the region."

The waste product is used as fertilizer for farms and golf courses as long as they don't use so much that it leaches into the ground. It can be processed into a fuel that can operate the machinery that transforms such inedible parts as the heads and feet into animal feed, or can be used to generate electricity.

You may drive past a chicken farm and from the smell of ammonia know where you are without even seeing anything. The Innovative Technology Fund—a partnership among the Maryland Department of Natural Resources, the University of Maryland, and the Environmental Protection Agency—has been working with AviHome of Salisbury to produce new ventilated plenum poultry house flooring. The plastic material is strong enough that machinery can be driven over it, eliminates the need for litter (wood shavings and sawdust), and allows enough air through that the moisture level in the fecal matter drops to as little as 20 percent, about half the moisture now. The drier manure and lack of litter reduces the amount of waste by at least 80 percent. If you'll recall from your old chemistry class, the ammonia-producing bacteria need a base pH and the flooring prevents the pH from going above seven, reducing the amount of ammonia.

Traditionally litter is placed on the floor, producing among other things ammonia, which is then ventilated by fan to the outside world. The chickens are okay, but if the weather happens to be funky, their waste helps produce smog and, well, you smell the results. Ammonia can also be a catalyst in the streams, rivers, and bay that starts an algae bloom that depletes the water of oxygen. When litter is removed from the equation, tons and tons of trees being harvested to create the litter are saved.

Dr. Jeannine Harter-Dennis, associate professor in the Department of Agriculture Food and Resource Science at the University of

Maryland Eastern Shore in Princess Anne, says she and the industry are aggressively pursuing this experiment because they would like to have something in place before the Environmental Protection Agency sets the guidelines, probably within the next ten years. Harper-Dennis sounds as excited as a child at a birthday party when she explains the benefits of this new flooring. Unfortunately, at the moment it's too expensive to produce to take the testing from trial to real application. Monies from grants and venture capitalists and angel investors have been requested.

AviHome calls the process a:

> . . . *win, win, win, win, win method for poultry production. The environment, the chickens, the farmer, the integrator, the consumer, the country, all benefit. The environment wins as it reduces litter, pollution, and waste. The chickens win as they're now living in a better, cleaner, drier environment breathing cleaner air. The farmer wins as his growout time and performance yields are improved. The integrator wins as they can now be more competitive in markets with a higher quality, lower cost product. The consumer wins as they now have a healthier product to consume. The country wins as thousands of jobs will be created to retrofit existing chicken houses as well as open new markets to export meat and AviHome systems.*

While the ammonia problem is being resolved, the US Department of Agriculture's Natural Resources Conservation Service, with the Maryland Department of Agriculture and the chicken farmers, has been installing vegetative buffers. Started in 2005, the buffer program includes trees, native grasses that tolerate drought, and irrigation systems that make the property more attractive, stop cold winter winds, and intercept ammonia and particulate emissions from the chicken houses. On July 13, 2011, additional funding was announced that provided for the planting of vegetative buffers on fifty additional chicken farms in the Chesapeake Bay Watershed. More than 250,000 trees have been planted through this program.

Any or all of these developments will have a great impact on the poultry business here, around the country, and throughout the world. The improved smell also will make the industry a better neighbor to the rapid population growth the Eastern Shore has and will continue to experience.

With almost every part of the chicken being used for something, the only thing left is the feathers. What does one do with the feathers from 600 million broiler chickens a year? That's about four billion pounds of feathers. Each and every year. Something has to be done with them.

On the one hand, most chickens are bred to have white feathers, so they don't have to be bleached to be used for stuffing and fluffing pillows and quilts. On the other hand, the feathers and quills are short and prickly, so they can work in inexpensive pillows (particularly those with a heavy, dense weave case), but they aren't as suitable as goose down for stuffing in expensive pillows and quilts and those with fine material and loose weaves.

A major breakthrough event came in 2000 when chemist Walter Schmidt at the Agriculture Research Service in Beltsville, Maryland, was working with polymer research scientist Justin Barone. Schmidt had been plucking around with feathers since the 1990s, first making them into decorative paper, filter papers, and similar products. Filters made with chicken feathers have finer pores than those made with wood pulp, thereby trapping more spores, dust, dander, and other allergens.

Then Schmidt pulverized the chicken feathers into powder, pushed them through an injection molder, and produced such things as biodegradable flowerpots. The pots degrade over a period of one to five years. Additionally, they consist of nitrogen, so they help enrich the soil. No petroleum is included in the recipe. It's a thermoplastic, so the material can be melted and recycled again and again as food package wrappings or plastic beverage ring holders. Imagine all those waterfowl that won't die because some careless beer drinker dropped a can-holder necklace into the bay.

Then, shortly after the turn of the twenty-first century, Schmidt and Barone combined quill fibers with plastic to make dashboards and other car parts that are lighter in weight, more durable, and better at noise absorption. Other applications for this fiber-plastic sound-deadening combination have been tested in office cubicles and sleeping areas of cabs used in towing large transport trailers.

So the next time you hear a rooster crowing the dawn, you can thank its relatives who gave their lives so you don't hear such noises in your car, office, and other quiet places.

STATE FACTS AND TRIVIA

- Statehood: April 28, 1788, the seventh state

- Capital: Annapolis

- Total Area: forty-second among states, 10,460 square miles

- Largest City: Baltimore

- Number of Counties: twenty-three

- Highest Point: Backbone Mountain, 1,024 meters (3,360 feet)

- Total Population: nineteenth among states

- The first dental school in the United States opened at the University of Maryland.

- Baltimore was home to the nation's first umbrella factory, the first coal-burning steam engine in 1830, and first elevated electric railway in 1893.

- Thirteen-year-old Edward Warren flew in the country's first successful manned balloon flight on June 24, 1784.

- The Maryland State House is the oldest state capitol still in continuous legislative use.

- The first practical refrigerator was invented in Baltimore in 1803.

- Channel 67 broadcast the state's first public television programs on October 5, 1969.

- The 1,200-foot Francis Scott Key Bridge in Baltimore is the second-longest continuous truss bridge in the nation.

- Baltimore is named after Cecil Calvert, who received the Maryland Colony from King Charles I. His title was Lord Baltimore.

- Annapolis, home of the US Naval Academy, has served as the state capital since 1694 and is one of the oldest settlements in Maryland.

- Nicknames: The Old Line State, the Free State, America in Miniature

- Greatest distance from north to south: 124 miles

- Greatest distance from east to west: 238 miles

- The Susquehanna River, primary source for the Chesapeake Bay, is the largest nonnavigable river in North America.

- State bird: Baltimore Oriole

- State boat: Skipjack

- State crustacean: Maryland blue crab

- State dinosaur: *Astrodon johnstoni*

- State dog: Chesapeake Bay retriever

- State drink: Milk

- State fish: Striped bass (rockfish)

- State flower: Black-eyed Susan

- State folk dance: Square dancing

- State fossil shell: *Ecphora quadricostata*

- State gem: Patuxent River stone

- State horse: Thoroughbred

- State insect: Baltimore checkerspot butterfly

- State motto: *Fatti Maschii, Parole Femine* (Manly Deeds, Womanly Words)

- State reptile: Diamondback terrapin

- State song: "Maryland, My Maryland"

- State sport: Jousting

- State team sport: Lacrosse

- State theaters: Center Stage, Baltimore; Olney Theater Center, Olney (summer theater)

- State tree: White oak

- State dessert: Smith Island Cake

- State cat: Calico

- Lots of people know that jousting is the Maryland state sport. Few know, however, that when it was selected in 1962, Maryland was the first to adopt a state sport. It took a few more years, until 2004, to adopt lacrosse as the state's official team sport.

- Still Pond, in Kent County, allowed women the right to vote in 1908, twelve years before the Nineteenth Amendment to the US Constitution was adopted. Of the fourteen women who cast a ballot, two were African American.

- Margaret Brent (1601–1671) moved from England to Maryland, near St. Mary's City, in 1639 with a sister and two brothers. She was the first woman in the colonies to act as an attorney before a court of the common law. Governor Leonard Calvert (Lord Baltimore) died suddenly in 1647, leaving only an oral will, naming Brent as executor of his estate. In 1648 she appeared before the Assembly and demanded to be admitted with two votes, one for herself as a landowner and one as Lord Baltimore's representative. She was denied.

- Maryland, like other states, has numerous organizational license plates, a concept that the state started by reserving blocks of regular-issue passenger plates for members of specific groups, reportedly as early as the 1920s. The practice was more defined in 1954 with such assignments as AL-00-00 for members of the American Legion. Such vanity plates do not pay any proceeds to the organization. Only two special plates provide such funding. One is the Chesapeake Bay plate, which provides money to the Chesapeake Bay Trust, and the other is the agricultural plate, which helps fund the Maryland Agricultural Education Foundation.

- In 1902 Maryland became the first state to enact a workers' compensation law. The law was considered unconstitutional because it did not allow workers to pursue their rights to a jury trial. Maryland Governor Phillips Lee Goldsborough in 1914 introduced another bill that did receive legislative and judicial approval. Today's law is basically the same as the one passed almost a century ago, with some amendments.

- St. Ignatius Church in Chapel Point, near Port Tobacco, has been around since Father Andrew White founded it in 1641, making it the oldest continuously serving Catholic parish in the country. Even in the days when the Jesuits were suppressed, from 1773 to 1814, the property and buildings were occupied. It's been known for some time that a tunnel existed between the slave quarters and the Port Tobacco River. However, most of the tunnel was filled in years ago. Father Salvador (Father or Padre Sal) Jordan, who was pastor there for twelve years, 1993–2005, says no one is sure whether the passage was to move slaves to and from boats, to move Jesuit priests to and from boats, or an easy and weatherproof way to transport supplies from the river up to the church.

- Thanksgiving (and thanks at other times of the year) go to the US Department of Agriculture/Agricultural Research Center at Beltsville. According to Sandy Miller Hays, director of information, "During the 1930s, people started having smaller families and they didn't need a turkey the size of a Shetland pony. The turkey was losing popularity, so we developed a smaller turkey, the Beltsville small white, in the 1940s that ranged from eight to ten pounds. It resuscitated the turkey industry. Now, pretty much every turkey—not wild turkeys—has at least some Small White genetics in its family tree."

BIBLIOGRAPHY

"1933 Chesapeake-Potomac Hurricane," www.enotes.com/topic/1933_Chesapeake%E2%80%93Potomac_hurricane.

"24 hours at Johns Hopkins," November 28, 2010, http://tricuspid.wordpress.com/category/blalock-taussig-shunt.

"Look What the Poultry Industry Is Doing for Delmarva," www.dpichicken.org/faq_facts/docs/FACTS10.doc.

1933 Hurricane/Tropical Data for Atlantic, www.weather.unisys.com/hurricane/atlantic/1933/index.html.

"A Pictorial History of Maryland License Plates," www.ricksplates.com/maryland/mdorg.htm.

Allen, Thomas B. *Harriet Tubman, Secret Agent: How Daring Slaves and Free Blacks Spied for the Union During the Civil War.* National Geographic Children's Books, 2006.

Ambrose, Kevin, Dan Henry, and Andy Weiss. *Washington Weather,* Historical Enterprises. 2002.

"Ammonia and the Environment," www.worldpoultry.net/editorial-opinion/ammonia-and-the-environment-8438.html.

"Army & Navy—Hagerstown Gets Hot." *Time,* July 13, 1942.

Atkinson, Steven G. "6 Things to Consider," http://6thingstoconsider.com/2008/08/23/the-great-hurricane-of-1933.

"Background Scene Plates," www.mva.maryland.gov/Vehicle-Services/REG/backgroundplate.htm.

Big Hearted Herbert. Internet Movie Database, www.imdb.com/title/tt0024892.

"Blalock-Taussig Shunt," http://en.wikipedia.org/wiki/Blalock-Taussig_shunt.

"Blue Baby Syndrome," http://en.wikipedia.org/wiki/Blue_baby_syndrome.

"Bookmobile Sunday Focuses on Importance of Mobile Outreach Services," http://americanlibrariesmagazine.org/news/ala/bookmobile-sunday-focuses-importance-mobile-outreach-services.

Butz, Natalie, news editor *The Elm* (student newspaper of Washington College), Spring 2010.

Chen, Li-Hui, Susan P. Baker, and Guohua Li. "Graduated Driver Licensing Programs and Fatal Crashes of 16-Year-Old Drivers: A National Evaluation," http://pediatrics.aappublications.org/content/118/1/56.full?sid=4f483113-fc92-4045-b19c-d4d335f090d6.

"Chesapeake-Potomac Hurricane—August 1933," www.hpc.ncep.noaa.gov/tropical/rain/chesapeakepotomac1933.html.

Clancy, Paul. "1933 Hurricane Slammed Unwarned Populace." *Virginian-Pilot,* August 18, 2008, http://hamptonroads.com/2008/08/1933-hurricane-slammed-unwarned-populace.

Coe, Lewis. *The Telegraph: A History of Morse's Invention and Its Predecessors in the United States.* Jefferson, NC: McFarland, 1993.

"Commanding General of MCRD Parris Island/ERR," www.mcrdpi.usmc.mil/leaders/CG.asp.

"Control of Ammonia in Poultry Litter Project Highlights," www.umes.edu/AES/Default.aspx?id=3516.

Courthenay, Walter R. Jr., and James D. Williams. "Snakeheads (Pisces, Channidae): A Biological Synopsis and Risk Assessment." Washington, DC: US Department of the Interior, US Geological Survey, 2004.

DeVincent-Hayes, Nan, and John E. Jacob. *Ocean City, Vol. 1 (Images of America: Maryland).* Mount Pleasant, SC: Arcadia Publishing, 1999.

Drucker, Malka, and Elizabeth Rosen. *Portraits of Jewish-American Heroes.* New York, NY: Dutton Children's Books, 2008.

"Duel of the Month Club: John F. Sherburne v. Daniel Key," *Ten Miles Square* blog, http://thetenmilessquare.blogspot.com/2009/06/duel-of-month-club-john-f-sherburne-v.html, accessed October 20, 2011.

"Facts About Maryland's Broiler Chicken Industry," www.dpichicken.org/faq_facts/docs/factsmd2009.doc.

Farquhar, Michael. *A Treasury of Great American Scandals.* New York, NY: Penguin Books, 2003.

Field, Mike. "Hopkins Pioneered 'Blue Baby' Surgery 50 Years Ago," *The Gazette* (Johns Hopkins University), November 29, 1994.

Flores, Alfredo. "Jefferson Trees Resistant to Dutch Elm Disease." US Department of Agriculture, July 12, 2006, www.ars.usda.gov/is/pr/2006/060613.htm.

Frankenfish. Internet Movie Database, www.imdb.com/title/tt0384833.

Friddell, Claudia and Troy Howell. *Goliath: Hero of the Great Baltimore Fire.* Ann Arbor, MI: Sleeping Bear Press, 2010.

Fullerton, Max. "The Day Frederick County Rebelled." *Baltimore Sunday Sun Magazine,* November 21, 1965, www.judgedavidlynn.org/The_Stamp_Act.html.

"Georges Creek Watershed Restoration Action Strategies Plan, Ideas for Today and Tomorrow," June 2002. http://www.mde .state.md.us/assets/document/wetlandswaterways/GA.pdf.

Global Harbors, http://globalharbors.org.

Goodheart, Adam. "Tea and Fantasy: Fact, Fiction and Revolution in an Historic American Town." *American Scholar,* Autumn 2005.

"Governor Martin O'Malley Requests Federal Funding for Eastern Shore Animal Health Diagnostic Laboratory and Cover Crops," March 11, 2010, www.gov.state.md.us/pressreleases/100311c .asp.

Greenberg, Robert A. *"Swish" Nicholson: A Biography of Wartime Baseball's Leading Slugger.* Jefferson, NC: McFarland, 2007.

Guy, Chris. "Reborn in a Hurricane." *Baltimore Sun,* August 23, 2006, www.baltimoresun.com/news/maryland/eastern-shore/bal-hurricane2003,0,7880742.story.

Hammond, John. "Dutch Elm Disease Update," *Agricultural Research,* June 2006, www.ars.usda.gov/is/AR/archive/jun06/ elm0606.htm.

Hayward, Mary Ellen, and Frank R. Shivers Jr., eds. *The Architecture of Baltimore: An Illustrated History.* Baltimore, MD: Johns Hopkins University Press, 2004.

"Helen Brooke Taussig." http://en.wikipedia.org/wiki/Helen_ Brooke_Taussig.

"Historic Hurricanes." www.hurricaneville.com/historic.html.

"Historic Light Station Information & Photography, Maryland." US Coast Guard, US Department of Homeland Security, www .uscg.mil/history/weblighthouses/LHMD.asp.

Holland, Barbara. *Gentlemen's Blood.* London: Bloomsbury Publishing, 2003.

Hubbes, M. "The American Elm and Dutch Elm Disease." *Forestry Chronicle* 72, no. 2 (March–April 1999).

Hudgins, C. Randolph Jr. *Tales of the '33 Hurricane (Norfolk, Virginia)*. Chapel Hill, NC: Fleet Publishing, 2001.

Kaplan, Kim. "Hidden Elm Population May Hold Genes to Combat Dutch Elm Disease." *Agricultural Research,* March 30, 2011, www.ars.usda.gov/is/pr/2011/110330.htm.

"Kiwifruit." http://en.wikipedia.org/wiki/Kiwifruit.

Kryzanowski, Tony. "Poultry Flooring System Yielding Positive Manure Management Results." *Manure Manager,* www.manuremanager.com/content/view/1951/38.

Kulling, Monica, and Teresa Flavin. *Escape North! The Story of Harriet Tubman*. New York: Random House Books for Young Readers, 2000.

Larson, Kate Clifford. *Bound for the Promised Land: Harriet Tubman, Portrait of an American Hero*. New York: Ballantine Books.

Lloyd, Alwyn T. *Fairchild C-82 Packet and C-119 Flying Boxcar.* Sittinghourne: Midland Publishing, 2005.

Madere, Louis E. *Railroads and Telecommunication.* Based on a legal research memorandum by Jean S. Ray, Baton Rouge, Louisiana, July 1995. www.madere.com/firstnet.htm.

"Maryland Workers' Compensation History," www.millerandzois.com/marylandworkerscomplawyer.html.

Matinee Theatre. Internet Movie Database, www.imdb.com/title/tt0047756.

McCullough, David. *The Greater Journey: Americans in Paris.* New York: Simon & Schuster, 2011.

Meade, Jennie C. "A Look Back at a Once-Legal Method of Resolving Disputes." *GW Law School Magazine,* George Washington University, Fall 2005.

Meyers, Kurtis. "A Heritage Awakened: The C-82 Comes Home." *New Pegasus 2,* no. 1 (Spring/Summer 2007).

Millspaugh, Martin L. "The Inner Harbor Story." *Urban Land,* April 2003.

Morgan, Edmund S., and Helen M. Morgan. *The Stamp Act Crisis: Prologue to Revolution.* Chapel Hill: University of North Carolina Press, 1995.

Musto, R. J. "The Treatment of the Wounded at Gettysburg: Jonathan Letterman: The Father of Modern Battlefield Medicine." *Gettysburg Magazine,* no. 37, 2007.

"National Bookmobile Day 2011," American Library Association, www.ala.org/ala/aboutala/offices/olos/nbdhome.cfm.

"Navy Policy Will Allow Women to Serve Aboard Submarines," US Navy, April 29, 2010, www.navy.mil/search/display .asp?story_id=52954.

Nelson, William E. *Common Law in Colonial America: Volume 1: The Chesapeake and New England, 1607–1660.* New York: Oxford University Press, 2008. www.bsos.umd.edu/gvpt/lpbr/ subpages/reviews/nelson0209.htm

"New American Elms Restore Stately Trees," *Agricultural Research,* July 1996, www.ars.usda.gov/is/AR/archive/jul96/elms0796. htm.

"Notable Graduates," US Naval Academy, www.usna.edu/ Admissions/Notables.

Olson, Sherry H. *Baltimore: The Building of an American City.* Baltimore, MD: Johns Hopkins University Press, 1997.

Pelton, Tom. "The Kerr, the Curse, and the $29,303 Writer: Brandon Hopkins Will Take the Money and Run to Escape the Supposed Curse of the Prize." *Baltimore Sun,* May 21, 1997.

Petersen, Peter B. *The Great Baltimore Fire,* Maryland Historical Society, 2005.

Pierson, Sandra. "Wicomico Public Library Unveils Bookmobile." *The Crab,* Spring 2007.

Pitts, Jonathan. "Where Medical Masterpieces Are Made." *Baltimore Sun,* July 17, 2011.

"Poultry Housing Technology Cuts Ammonia." www .worldpoultry.net/news/poultry-housing-technology-cuts-ammonia-id591.html.

"Poultry Waste to Power Energy Plant." www.worldpoultry.net/ news/poultry-waste-to-power-energy-plant-7865.html.

Raitz, Karl B., et al., eds. *The National Road.* Baltimore, MD: Johns Hopkins University Press, 1996; online edition.

"Rear Admiral Michelle Howard." US Navy Biography, www.navy .mil/navydata/bios/navybio.asp?bioID=394.

"Recommendations for Flood Damage Reduction—Westernport Elementary School." Maryland Department of Natural Resource and Baltimore District, US Army Corps of Engineers, 1989.

"Repudiation Day." http://encyclopedia2.thefreedictionary.com/ Repudiation+Day.

"Reynolds, Brigadier General Loretta E." https://slsp.manpower .usmc.mil/gosa/biographies/rptBiography.asp?PERSON_ ID=3180&PERSON_TYPE=General.

Rinehart, Theron K. *Yesterday, Today, Tomorrow: Fifty Years of Fairchild Aviation.* Hagerstown, MD: Fairchild Hiller Corp., 1971.

Samenow, Jason. "75 Years Since Chesapeake Potomac Hurricane." *Capital Weather Gang* blog, August 23, 2008, http://voices .washingtonpost.com/capitalweathergang/2008/08/75_years_ since_great_1933_hurr.html.

Schwartz, Rick. *Hurricanes and the Middle Atlantic States: A Surprising History . . . From Jamestown to the Present.* Blue Diamond, NV: Blue Diamond Books, 2007.

Seck, Momar D., and David D. Evans. *Major U.S. Cities Using National Standard Fire Hydrants, One Century After the Great Baltimore Fire.* National Institute of Standards and Technology, August 2004.

"Seven Foot Knoll Lighthouse." www.lighthousefriends.com/light .asp?ID=419.

Shirley, Glennor. "Bookmobiles for Maryland Correctional Education Libraries Arrive." *The Crab,* Summer 2007.

Shomette, Donald G. *Ghost Fleet of Mallow's Bay.* Lanaster, PA: Schiffer Publishing, 1996; www.dnr.state.md.us/naturalresource/ winter2001/ghostship.html.

Snakehead Terror. Internet Movie Database, www.imdb.com/title/ tt0371954.

"Sophie Kerr." Internet Movie Database, www.imdb.com/name/ nm0449805.

Standage, Tom. *The Victorian Internet: The Remarkable Story of the Telegraph and Nineteenth Century's On-line Pioneers.* Walker & Company, 2007.

Stegman, Carolyn B. *Women of Achievement in Maryland History.* 2002.

Stein, Mark. *How the States Got Their Shapes.* Washington, DC: Smithsonian, 2008.

"Tetralogy of Fallot." http://en.wikipedia.org/wiki/Tetralogy_of_ Fallot.

"Think You Know About Graduated Driver Licensing Programs?" www.jhsph.edu/publichealthnews/press_releases/2006/baker_ gdlquiz.html.

Thomas, James W., and Thomas J. C. Williams. *History of Allegany County, Maryland.* Baltimore, MD: Regional Publishing Co., 1926.

"Timeline of John Hanson's Life, Roles in the Birth of the United States, Presidency and Remembrances Since His Death." www .johnhansonmemorial.org/index_files/John_Hanson_Timeline .pdf.

Titcomb, Mary Lemist. *A County Library: And on the Trail of the Book Wagon, Papers Read at the Meeting of the American Library Association.* Herald Pub. Co., June 1909.

Touart, Paul Baker. *Along the Seaboard Side: The Architectural History of Worcester County, Maryland.* Snow Hill, MD: Worcester County Library, 1994.

———. *Somerset: An Architectural History.* Baltimore, MD: Maryland Historical Trust Press, 1990.

"UMES, MD Hawk Corp., and AviHome Partner to Build Poultry Houses of the Future" University of Maryland, Eastern Shore, 2011. www.umes.edu/PR/Article.aspx?id=3220.

"Vintage Buildings: Department Stores: 3H's and an S." *Monumental City,* www.monumentalcity.net/buildings/ deptstores.

"Why the West Side Matters: Read's Drug Store and Baltimore's Civil Rights Heritage." Baltimore Heritage, January 7, 2011, www.baltimoreheritage.org/2011/01/why-the-west-side-matters-reads-drug-store-and-baltimores-civil-rights-heritage.

Woodring, Frank, and Suanne Woodring. *Fairchild Aircraft.* Mount Pleasant, SC: Arcadia Publishing, 2007.

INDEX

INDEX

ABOUT THE AUTHOR

Judy Colbert is a native Washingtonian (D.C., not the state) who has traveled the mid-Atlantic area extensively since childhood.

"I went on school field trips as I was growing up, and then I was the room mother for my daughters' field trips," she says. "All the teachers knew they could call on me to chaperone, regardless of which class it was. Okay, I did tire of the bread bakery and the potato chip factory, and for a while even the zoo. I have a mental picture of French rugrats sitting in the Hall of Mirrors in Versailles (circa 1624) and American rugrats doing the same thing in the US Capitol. Now, sightseeing with my granddaughters lets me enjoy the life and loves of this area through still other eyes.

"One great thing (among many) about living in this area is *everyone* comes to visit and that means I go sightseeing with my friends and family. I can always find something new or different and I love that much of my writing involves taking off and exploring. I'm innately curious and I've always thought that I've been given a great opportunity enjoying that curiosity."

A natural-born storyteller who has honed her craft for many years, Judy is thrilled when someone says, "I didn't know that," about a place that's right down the street or across the county line. Judy likes to wander into diners, libraries, and even beauty parlors to listen to the locals as they tell her to "Go talk to Uncle Fred. He invented the wooden leg." "I don't know if that's true or they're pulling *my* leg," she says. "It doesn't matter."

Judy is an award-winning writer and photographer who is the author of *Maryland and Delaware Off the Beaten Path; Virginia Off the Beaten Path; Insiders' Guide to Baltimore; Chesapeake Bay Crabs*

Cookbook; Country Towns of Maryland and Delaware; Fun Places to Go with Children in Washington, D.C.; Peaceful Places Washington, D.C.; and the forthcoming *It Happened in Delaware* and *It Happened in Arkansas.* She has written hundreds, if not thousands, of articles that have appeared in international, national, regional, and local publications and websites, including the *Howard County Times* and www.FreeFunGuides.com.

After thoroughly exploring the mid-Atlantic, Judy would like to spend a year or two on a cruise ship exploring other parts of the world. She is a member of the American Society of Authors and Journalists, Society of Professional Journalists, Screen Actors Guild, and American Federation of Television Arts and Sciences.

Want **More** Maryland?

Check out this other great title by Judy Colbert and published by GPP:

Maryland and Delaware Off the Beaten Path

Introduction

Welcome to *Maryland and Delaware Off the Beaten Path,* ninth edition, two states where you'll find some of the best food, the friendliest people, the most incredible history, amazingly unusual attractions, wonderful scenery and natural resources, and enough interesting ways to spend a few hours off the interstate to keep you busy for years.

Maryland is often called America in Miniature because the state goes from the seashore (the Atlantic Ocean and the Chesapeake Bay) on the east to the mountains (the Appalachians) on the west. The mountains are not high compared to the Rockies (Backbone Mountain in Garrett County is the tallest, at 3,360 feet), but they provide fair downhill and excellent cross-country skiing. The seashore is among the finest in the East. In one day you can go from one to the other and theoretically ski in the morning and the afternoon; snow skiing one direction, water skiing the other. About the only clime we don't have here is desert, yet there are sand quarries.

Not everything in Maryland, however, is miniature. The National Aquarium in Baltimore is one of the world's largest. The collection at the Walter's Art Museum, also in Baltimore, is world renowned. Maryland also has one of the nation's largest hydroelectric generating stations at Conowingo (Cecil County), the largest colony of African black-footed penguins in the United States (Baltimore City Zoo), one of the largest and finest public libraries in the United States at the Enoch Pratt Free Library (Baltimore City), and the largest wooden dome in the country built without nails (Annapolis). Well, the list continues, but you get the idea.

Maryland is also called the Free State (road signs say KEEP THE FREE STATE LITTER FREE), and if you ask residents, they'd probably cite the freedom of worship advocated by the state's founders. Others might point to Maryland's alliance with the northern states during "the war" and its intolerance of slavery (at least in some parts of the state). These historical facts are true, but the nickname dates from 1917, when the state opposed Prohibition on the grounds that it was a states' rights issue.

And a third nickname is the Old Line State, which honors Maryland's regular line troops who served courageously in the Revolutionary War.

In the summer of 2000, Maryland introduced its Scenic Byways program, celebrating the "roads less traveled." From the mountains to the seashore, nineteen scenic byways have been designated, encompassing 2,487 miles. The average length of a byway is 60 miles and takes seventy minutes to drive, but lots of side trips are possible. The shortest is five miles, along the Historic National Seaport route, and the longest is 170 miles along the Historic National Road route. As part of this program, 800 new SCENIC BYWAYS signs were erected, a state map was created, and a free 192-page book titled *Maryland Scenic Byways* was published. For information, contact the state highway administration communications office at (410) 545-0303 or (800) 323-6742. You can download a PDF version of the scenic byways map at www.marylandroads.com/oed/MarylandScenicByways.pdf. The Chesapeake Country Byway, the only National Scenic Byway in Maryland and one of only seventy-five in the country, runs from Stevensville (through Chestertown) to Chesapeake City, with legs to Rock Hall and the Eastern Neck National Wildlife Refuge.

official fossil

The state's official fossil, the four-ribbed snail, is an extinct invertebrate that ranged in size from microscopic to three or four inches in diameter. Fossils can be found at the Cliffs of Calvert, in the Choptank and St. Mary's areas.

Two historic trails let you explore some of the highlights of the Civil War and the War of 1812. The **Civil War Trail** includes carefully mapped driving tours that explore the Antietam campaign, John Wilkes Booth's escape from Ford's Theatre after assassinating President Abraham Lincoln, and Baltimore. The **Star Spangled Banner Trail & The War of 1812** is a 100-mile scenic and historic trail that follows the route taken by the British Marines as they invaded the Chesapeake Bay area in 1814.

Maryland is also involved with the Gateways Network, coordinated by the National Park Service in partnership with the Chesapeake Bay program. A Gateway is an entrance to the byways and water trails in the National Park Service program. Among the first Chesapeake Bay Gateways in Maryland, Washington, D.C., Virginia, Pennsylvania, and New York, are twelve Gateway sites, one Gateway hub, two regional information centers, seven water trails, and one land trail. And, that's just the beginning. Pick a Maryland Gateway and you may visit the Barge House Museum (Annapolis), the Blackwater National Wildlife Refuge (Cambridge), Jefferson Patterson Park and Museum

(St. Leonard), and the Monocacy River Water Trail. For additional information, stop by www.baygateways.net.

Maryland toll roads are part of the E-Z Pass system (all of New England except Vermont and Connecticut, and west to Chicago, Illinois and south to Virginia and West Virginia) that lets you through toll booths by collecting tolls electronically. Maryland and DRBA (Delaware River and Bay Authority) collect a monthly account maintenance fee ($1.50) and an initial fee.

Maryland has four area codes divided in an overlay pattern. Generally, 301 and 240 codes are for the western, suburban Maryland (around Washington, D.C.), and southern Maryland counties. Similarly, 410 and 443 are for Annapolis, Baltimore, and Eastern Shore areas. All local calls require the entire ten-digit number (area code and phone number). Only long-distance calls require the number 1 before the ten-digit number.

Although much of Maryland is urban, you can find open countryside within a few miles of wherever you are. You can also find campgrounds and the National Association of RV Parks and Campgrounds recognized Jellystone Park Camp-Resort in Williamsport with its "Plan-It-Green" Award and the Maryland Association of Campgrounds

howtoflytheflag

The Maryland flag was adopted in 1904. The red and white section is the coat of arms of the Crossland family, the first Lord Baltimore's relatives on his mother's side. The black and gold design is the coat of arms for the Calvert family, Lord Baltimore's relatives on his father's side. When hanging the flag, the black and gold quadrant is uppermost and closest to the pole.

won an award for producing the best statewide campground direction in the small state category in 2009. Deb Carter of the Maryland Association of Campgrounds was selected as the "State Executive Director of the Year." For additional information, call (303) 681-0401 or visit www.GoCampingAmerica.com.

In addition to showcasing Maryland's attractions, this book also explores Delaware, which has been called Small Wonder for its diminutive size and its natural beauty. Only 96 miles in length, the state is bordered by the Atlantic Ocean and Delaware Bay on the east and Maryland to the west and south. Delaware proudly boasts the fact that there is no sales tax. That's why you'll find so many outlet stores and other good shopping venues, from small shops to sprawling malls, throughout the state.

The area code for Delaware is 302, and you needn't dial it for local calls within Delaware.

I hope you enjoy reading and using this book as much as I enjoy discovering *Maryland and Delaware Off the Beaten Path*.

CAPITAL REGION

Prince George's, Montgomery, and Frederick Counties make up the Greater Washington area. Washington, D.C. is at the center of a huge suburban megalopolis formed by the blending of these three counties and northern Virginia. Although some areas are densely populated with seemingly miles upon miles of row or town houses, you can also find miles and miles of parkland, green spaces, and farm lands. Because so many people who live here come from other places, such as places where it never snows, traffic seems to get jammed as soon as the TV and radio weather forecasters think about snow. Forget about what happens when it actually does snow. If you should be here when it snows, tune in to a radio or TV station, and go for public transportation. Or find a nice fireplace and cuddle up with a good book.

As a native of this area, I have enjoyed visitors from all over the world who want to tour Washington. I take them to the subway station, and the Metro Rail takes them downtown to the many Smithsonian buildings, galleries, the zoo, or anything else they want to see. The Washington Metro is as clean and safe as any subway system around and at last count was the second busiest subway in the country.

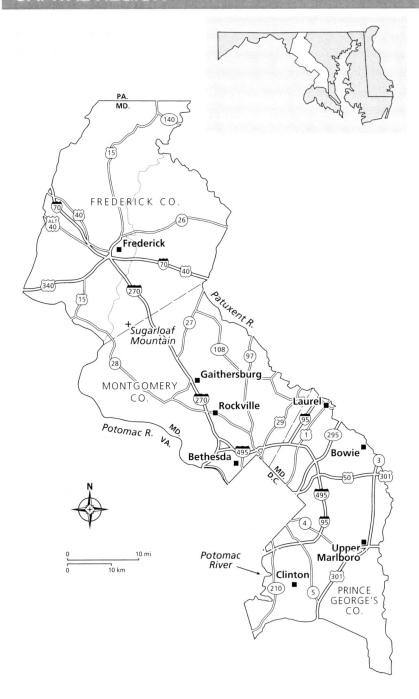

Metro lines are designated by color and by final destination. So, the Orange line has one terminus at New Carrollton, in Maryland, and Vienna/Fairfax-GMU is the other terminus, in Virginia. Check the map at www.wmata.com/rail/maps/map.cfm. If you catch an Orange line train at New Carrollton or some other station between there and your destination (say, Smithsonian), then you want to look for an Orange line train with a New Carrollton destination when you return. Complicating that a little bit is the fact that the Orange and Blue lines both stop at some stations. If you're boarding at Stadium-Armory to go to Capital South, you can ride either the Blue or Orange line train.

trackthe escaperoute

In the spring and the fall, the Mary Surratt Society sponsors a "Booth's Trail" tour that follows the path of John Wilkes Booth from Ford's Theatre in Washington, D.C., to Dr. Mudd's home, to the Garrett Farm in northern Virginia. These fascinating tours fill up quickly, and reservations are essential. Call (301) 868-1121 for tour dates and information.

Three lines run in Prince George's County: the Green, the Orange, and the Blue. Green line stations are at Greenbelt, College Park, Prince George's Plaza, West Hyattsville, Branch Ave., Suitland, and Naylor Rd.; Orange line stations are at New Carrollton, Landover, and Cheverly; and Blue line stations are at Addison Rd., Capitol Heights, Morgan Blvd, and Largo Town Center.

In Montgomery County, the Red line runs somewhat parallel to itself, with one terminus at Glenmont and the other one at Shady Grove. The middle of the Red line is Metro Center. The Shady Grove line has stations at Shady Grove, Rockville, Twinbrook, White Flint, Grosvenor, Medical Center, Bethesda, and Friendship Heights going in toward Washington. The Glenmont line has stations at Takoma Park, Silver Spring, Forest Glen, Wheaton, and Glenmont. In both the Prince George's and Montgomery station listings, those

AUTHOR'S FAVORITES CAPITAL REGION

College Park Aviation Museum

Mount Olivet Cemetery

Patuxent Research Refuge

Roddy Road Covered Bridge

U.S. Department of Agriculture Research Center

White's Ferry

are the stations within each county, not all of the stations on each line as they enter Washington, D.C.

Basically, trains run Mon through Thurs from 5 a.m. to midnight and until 3 a.m. on Fri night. On Sat and Sun, the stations open at 7 a.m. However, the last train may depart the station before it is officially closed. Operating hours are extended for such things as the fireworks on the Mall or the Marine Marathon. In other words, check the Web site, www.wmata.com for current schedules.

One more thought about taking Metro downtown for sightseeing. What appears to be the "best" station isn't always so. If you're going to the National Gallery of Art, you probably will do better going to the Archives-Navy Memorial-Penn Quarter station than going to the Smithsonian station. Additionally, some entrances are closed on weekends, so you want to know where you're going when you're going. Once you do this, Metro is a piece of cake. Just don't eat or drink while you're in the stations or on the trains.

Public art can be found at many Metro stations thanks to the MetroArts program. In Montgomery County, stop at the Glenmont station to see Deirdre Saunder's glass mosaic frieze *Swallows and Stars* (2001) and the Wheaton station to see Marcia F. Billig's bronze sculpture *The Commute* (1994). Sally Calmer's *Penguins Rush Hour*, which should be on display at the Silver Spring station, is in storage during construction. See more details in the Silver Spring section. Prince George's County Metro stations include art by Heidi Lippman with Ben Van Dusen, who created the glass and stone mosaic frieze *Dawn and Dusk* (1999) at the New Carrollton station; Ray King, who made the stainless steel and glass sculpture *Largo Beacon* (2004) at the Largo Town Center Station; Athena Tacha, who fashioned the sculpture *Stop & Go For Garrett A. Morgan* (2004) at the Morgan Blvd station; George Peters and Melanie Walker, who did the neon wall sculpture *Light Wheel* (2004); and Clark Weigman, whose painted metal and glass sculpture *Departure* (2004) is at the Branch Ave. station. Oh, by the way, Garrett Morgan is credited with inventing a type of traffic signal.